# The Little Hi... Rotterdam f...

Cheat Sheet

## Crucial Years and

**Around 1270**
Damming of the river Rotte, rise ...

**1299**
Town charter granted by Wolfert van Borselen

**1340**
Town charter granted by Count Willem IV

**1466**
Birth of Erasmus

**1590-1615**
First major harbor expansion

**1769**
Foundation of the Batavian Society for Experimental Philosophy

**1832**
Crooswijk General Cemetery used for the first time

**1872**
Opening of the shipping canal Nieuwe Waterweg

**From 1875**
Second major harbor expansion

**May 14, 1940**
Destruction of the center of Rotterdam as a result of German bombardments

**1950**
Reconstruction manifestation in Rotterdam Ahoy'

**1962-2004**
Rotterdam, the biggest port in the world

**March 16, 2010**
Rozenburg becomes the twelfth sub-municipality of Rotterdam

**May 14, 2010**
Demarcation of the 12-kilometer long fire boundary

**2014**
Van Nelle Factory receives UNESCO World Heritage Status

# *The Little History of Rotterdam for Dummies*

**Wilma van Giersbergen**
**René Spork**
**Translation: Barbara Stuart**

BBNC uitgevers

**Amersfoort, 2016**

ISBN: 978-90-453-5170-4
NUR: 693
Keywords: Rotterdam, history

This is a publication of BBNC uitgevers bv, Amersfoort
www.bbnc.nl
www.dummies.nl

Typesetting and cover: Imago Mediabuilders, Amersfoort
Printing and binding: Ten Brink bv, Meppel

# Table of Contents

# Introduction

The period between the foundation of the simple settlement Rotta and the creation of world port Rotterdam spans a thousand years of history. If we look at the prehistoric period (finds on the plains of the Maas estuary) we might even go back in time some 150,000 years, as far as traces of habitation are concerned. Can all that be contained in one little book, a booklet for dummies? Dummies meaning interested people but not necessarily trained historians, people who would like to learn about the history of Rotterdam in outline, with lots of fun facts?

To answer this question: yes it can. The proof is in your hands right now.

## Precursors

Being concise is only possible if you can build on the work of your predecessors. First of all these are: *Stad in aanwas. Geschiedenis van Rotterdam tot 1813* by Arie van der Schoor *(Town in Growth: History of Rotterdam until 1813)* and *Stad van Formaat. Geschiedenis van Rotterdam in de negentiende en twintigste eeuw* by Paul van de Laar *(A Great City: History of Rotterdam in the Nineteenth and Twentieth Century).* These books successively appeared in 1999 and 2000 as two parts of a city history. The concise *Het Rotterdam Boek* (2005) by Arie van der Schoor is more or less based on these two parts (*Book of Rotterdam*, published in 2010).

Was this the end of the history of Rotterdam? By no means! In light of the disastrous bombardment of May 14, 1940, a separate book about the war was deemed appropriate. Thus the book *Rotterdam in de Tweede Wereldoorlog* appeared in 2006, *Rotterdam in the Second World War* by Hans van der Pauw, consisting of 956 pages and weighing three kilograms.

This still didn't wrap up the complete history of Rotterdam. By then a national discussion was held regarding the so-called canon. History had to be captured in fifty 'windows', being the main historical themes. Rotterdam went for it as well and therefore its canon was published in 2011: *Geschiedenis van Rotterdam. De canon van het Rotterdams Verleden* by Els van den Bent in collaboration with the authors of this little *For Dummies (History of Rotterdam: the canon of the Past of Rotterdam)*. In that same year, Els van den Bent also published the commercial edition of her dissertation: *Proeftuin Rotterdam: droom en daad tussen 1975-2005* (literally translated: experimental garden Rotterdam: dream and act between 1975 and 2005).

So was this it, then? Eh, not really. It is said that Rotterdam is a city that is never really finished, which certainly applies to its history. Critics who had studied the two parts of the city's history mentioned above, noted that it had been written from the perspective of Rotterdam, but they wondered what the rise of Rotterdam had meant for the neighboring villages that were gradually swallowed up by the port city. Arie van der Schoor was willing to do research, resulting in a publication – in 2013 – about the villages of Rotterdam, from origins to annexation *(De dorpen van Rotterdam: van ontstaan tot annexatie)*.

We certainly shouldn't forget the young people of Rotterdam. In 2015, Ruud Spruit published his book *Mijn Stad Rotterdam (My City Rotterdam)*, a journey through history in seventeen stories for young and old, with a preface by Mayor Aboutaleb.

All's well that ends well? We've covered the war by now, but what about the period of rebuilding? In the fall of 2015, historians Anne Jongstra and Arie van der Schoor, both from the Municipal Archives of Rotterdam, presented their photo book on the reconstruction called *Rotterdam 1945-1970*, and then we have not even mentioned the three historic volumes about soccer club Feyenoord, by Jan Oudenaarden.

# About This Book

As mentioned, this book contains a history in outlines. Like to know more? Check out the aforementioned titles and don't forget to actually go into the city. Because despite the bombing, history is certainly visible in the city; from Delfshaven and the statue of Erasmus to the marking of the fire boundary by little lights in the sidewalk and streets (a ribbon stretching a distance of 12 km). See further: www.stadsarchief.rotterdam

# Icons Used in This Book

The margins of this book are provided with icons to emphasize the contents of the text of a particular paragraph. The followings icons have been used.

This icon signifies major events in the history of Rotterdam.

This icon emphasizes that the paragraph describes an important development.

This icon indicates an anecdote or 'nice to know' information about Rotterdam's history.

This icon lets you know that an historical figure or visitor has been quoted.

## Chapter 1

# What Preceded Rotterdam (ca. 150.000 B.C. – A.D. 1570)

### *In This Chapter:*

- Oldest human remains
- Drowned and resurrected Rotta
- Battle against the water
- The three 'Schieën'
- Fat herring and ruined castles
- Erasmus Roterodamus

Hunters and fishermen settle in the Maas estuary. Around the year 1000 there is already a settlement named Rotta, an important trading hub. Massive floods at the end of the twelfth century put an end to Rotta. A dam in the river Rotte, built around 1270, offers a solution and a new Rotta is created on the dam. By the time Rotterdam receives the town charter in 1340, allowing the building of a shipping canal to the Schie, trading can begin.

## Living in the Meuse Estuary

About 10,000 years ago, the delta of the river Meuse was inhabited by hunters and fishermen. Evidence for this is provided by spear points and harpoon and arrowheads – made of bone and antler – from the Middle Stone Age (ca. 8,000-6,000 B.C.). Traces of a permanent settlement were also found in Rotterdam itself. At a depth of twelve meters below the Central Station, traces of habitation were found; a piece of string and some food remains dating to 5,500 B.C. The Bureau of Archaeological Research of the City of Rotterdam (BOOR) uncovered a fire place and flint tools from the same era in Beverwaard near IJsselmonde. The location also yielded three cremation pits with burnt human remains from approximately 7,500-7,000 B.C. People lived in the Meuse estuary up until the Bronze Age (2,000-800 B.C.). The hunters and fishermen gradually shifted to the practice of farming but the inhabitants moved away because it was actually too wet for this. During the Iron Age (800-112 B.C.) the area of the current city of Rotterdam was again occupied by farmers.

DID YOU KNOW?

### Oldest find

The oldest find in the Rotterdam area stems from the beach of Oostvoorne near the Meuse delta (Maasvlakte). It is a flint plane that was used between 150,000 and 50,000 years ago by a Neanderthal individual during the Old Ice Age.

### Human burials

The human cremation remains that were found in three pits during an excavation in the Rotterdam district Beverwaard, are about 9,000 years old. These are the oldest dated human graves of the Netherlands. They were situated in a river dune; a high, dry place in the swamps. The age of the deceased individuals is between 10 and 40 years. Associated objects were found, such as flint tools, a stone hammer and a grindstone. The excavation was carried out by BOOR in 2008.

## International Hub

In Roman times the area was densely populated and there were hundreds of farms. The presence of the Roman army stimulated the demand for agricultural products. People tried to control the water levels by building wooden locks and digging trenches and ditches. There were many busy markets and an intensive international trade, attested by archaeological finds such as coins, glass, roof tiles and imported pottery. The area was depopulated in the second half of the third century when the Roman Empire fell apart, but also because the area was getting increasingly waterlogged.

## Drowned Rotta

The settlement called Rotta developed on the clay banks along the estuary of the river Rotte. It was part of the Meuse estuary, which was an important junction between England, Scandinavia and Germany. Rotta was an agricultural settlement and a link in this trade route. Its importance is demonstrated by the fact that it already had a parish church around 1028. Massive floods put an end to Rotta. The reclamation of land along the Rotte shifted further inland, where new settlements came into being. More dams were built along the rivers and more and more land was brought under cultivation. Thus emerged in the thirteenth century the polders Blommersdijk and Cool on the west side of the river Rotte, and on the east side the polder Voor-Rubroek. Several village communities developed. Kralingen is first mentioned as a parish in 1270, and the history of the Hillegonda-church in Hillegersberg is at least as old.

## The Dam in the River Rotte: Rotterdam

KEY MOMENT

The construction of the dam in the Rotte, around 1270, completed the series of embankments along the Nieuwe Maas (New Meuse). Elongated polders stretched out on both sides of the river Rotte, where one day the city of Rotterdam would arise. The 400-meter long dam is located on the site of the present Hoogstraat (High Street). After the Medieval Period it was called Middeldam (Middle Dam). It was fitted with wooden sluices to discharge the excess water from the surrounding countryside. Gradually, people started building on the dam and actually living there. Around 1300, several houses stood in the middle of the dam on a kind of low mound called 'terp' in Dutch. The dam was inhabited by no more than a few hundred people, mostly fishermen, artisans and landowners. Shortly after that period, people started building north of the dam, on either side of the Rotte. The name Rotterdam is first mentioned in the list of 'loans' of Count Floris V, dating to 1281-1284. The Middeldam was the heart of the city. During the fourteenth century, the Sint-Laurenskerk (St. Lawrence's Church) and the so-called Guest House (serving as a hospital) were constructed nearby. The settlement was owned by the count, for whom an inn was built where he stayed when he was in Rotterdam. Well into the fourteenth century, the dam was raised and expanded several times and until 1941 it remained the only high embankment in Rotterdam.

# *Battle against the Water: the Water Boards*

Rotterdam has different soil structures north and south of the Maas. The north consists of peat while the south has clay-on-peat. This led to the use of various construction methods. Common was the fight against the water. At the end of the twelfth century, a large part of the surrounding land had been reclaimed. Polders with embankments were constructed and windmills were installed to take care of the drainage. The main river embankment in the area of Schieland was that along the north bank of the Nieuwe Maas. This embankment would later be known as Schielands Hoge Zeedijk (the high sea embankment of Schieland), dating to the end of the twelfth century. It was maintained by adjacent landowners. The mouths of the rivers Schie and Rotte into the Nieuwe Maas formed the only breaks in the embankment. To prevent flooding, dams with locks were placed in these rivers. Stakeholders from different polders and crafts joined hands for this job. Thus, the water management turned from a local affair into a supra-local job, ultimately leading to the establishment of a special organization: the water board (hoogheemraadschap). It was headed by the bailiff, now called 'dijkgraaf' (literally meaning count of the dike, official English equivalent is the title of dike reeve) who took care of all water-related issues in the area together with the other parties concerned.

DID YOU KNOW?

## Town charter

The town charter (also called city charter), which was a privilege, was received by the surrounding towns of Dordrecht, Delft and Vlaardingen respectively in 1220, 1246 and 1273. Rotterdam did not receive her town charter until March 17, 1299, from the hands of Wolfert van Borselen, only to lose it again soon afterwards. Van Borselen wanted – together with Rotterdam – to strengthen his position against Dordrecht and Schiedam, which were not on his side. On August 1, 1299, he was murdered in Delft. Rotterdam's city charter was revoked shortly after that.

Rotterdam was given 'royal' privileges on July 25th, 1328, by Count Willem III. The real city charter was obtained on June 7, 1340. It was granted by Count Willem IV, but the people of Rotterdam had to pay for it. For the nearly 2,000 inhabitants at that time it yielded a number of privileges, such as toll freedom in the county of Holland, exemption from some taxes and greater powers in the fields of administration and justice. On the other hand, the population was obliged to provide troops in case of war and had to pay some other taxes.

DID YOU KNOW?

## Delft as competitor

Although Rotterdam was favorably situated along the Nieuwe Maas and the river Rotte, it did not have a shipping link with other Dutch cities. This changed as a result of being granted the town charter in 1340: the city was allowed to dig a shipping canal from Rotterdam to the Schie at Overschie. The Rotterdam Schie was finished in 1350, connecting the rivers Rotte and Schie and thereby ensuring a passage to Delft, and even further to Leiden and Haarlem. In 1389, because Delft was afraid of competition, it was given permission by Albrecht of Bavaria, the count of Holland, to dig another canal from the Schie near Overschie to the Nieuwe Maas. The new canal was called the 'Delfshavense Schie' and thus Delfshaven, or the port of Delft, was born. Since there was also a water connection between Overschie and Schiedam, called the 'Schiedamse Schie', from that moment on people spoke of the 'Drie (three) Schieën'.

## Herring: Source of Income

Besides functioning as a drainage system for the surrounding countryside, the river Rotte also served as a trade connection between Antwerp, Bruges, England, Scotland, France and the Baltic region. The ships could moor at the 'Steyger' (pier or quay). The dam prevented a direct passage and skippers had to reload their goods or temporarily store them, thus creating a staple market or staple port.

Fishing for herring became a major source of income. Herring was caught using special herring boats called 'buizen' (herring buss). During the fifteenth century, Rotterdam and Schiedam were among the main landing and staple ports of herring. The herring, which could be stored for longer thanks to the technique of herring curing (haring kaken) was mainly exported. For international trade, the city also had merchant ships. In the sixteenth century, these ships transported goods from the Baltic region – pitch, tar, grain and timber – to France, from which they returned with grain and wine. Traditionally, there were also overseas business contacts with England and Scotland, and in the southern Netherlands with Antwerp and Bruges. The emergence of Rotterdam as a trading and merchant city pushed fishing for herring to the background.

## Castles in Ruins

Thanks to the violent encounters between the Hoeken (Hooks) and Kabeljauwen (Cods) Rotterdam has very few castles. This power struggle within the Dutch nobility took place roughly between 1350 and 1490. The fight was mainly about succession, such as that of Jacoba van Beieren (Bavaria, she belonged to the Hook-faction), who succeeded her father but was not recognized as countess of Holland by her uncle Jan van Beieren who belonged to the faction of the Cods (Kabeljauwen). After Jan's death the struggle continued, but now between Jacoba and Philip the Good. This led to widespread destruction in Holland. When the Treaty of Delft was signed in 1428, Jacoba subjected to Philip, but until then looting was the order of the day. For that reason Rotterdam had received permission in 1358 to fortify the city, resulting in the digging of the canal called Coolsingel and the construction of defense works. Still, Squire Frans van Brederode – of the Hook faction – managed to seize Rotterdam in 1488 with an army of about 850 men. Seven months later – in exchange for free passage – he handed over the city to Governor Jan van Egmond. The surrounding countryside continued to suffer from raids by the roaming gangs of the Hooks, as a result of which the castles Ter Spangen, Spangenberg and Starrenburg in the so-called Spangense Polder were destroyed, as were the medieval castles Rodenrijs, Honingen and Weena.

## Erasmus Roterodamus

The famous writer, scholar and humanist Desiderius Erasmus (1466-1536) was born in Rotterdam and died in Basel. As a toddler Erasmus left the city, never to return again. Although he spent the rest of his life mainly abroad, he felt connected to Rotterdam and from 1506 onwards he called himself Desiderius Erasmus Roterodamus. His most famous publication, *Lof der Zotheid* (Praise of Folly), is a satire on the abuses of that era. In this publication Erasmus opposes all possible outward forms of religious practice. Thanks to the printing press Erasmus' work was known throughout Europe into the highest circles. During his lifetime he was already a famous scholar.

### Birthplace of Erasmus

Erasmus was born in his grandmother's house, in the vicinity of the St. Laurenskerk (St. Lawrence Church). After his death, the family house became a place of pilgrimage. However, it did change in the course of time. The house was first provided with a stepped gable, later a bell-gable and even later still a façade with a straight cornice. In 1895, the house was transformed into a large warehouse along with the two adjacent buildings. Out of respect, the owner built a faux-façade against the façade of his new warehouse. This 'old' façade received much appreciation since it was built in the spirit of the times in which Erasmus lived. In 1911, the warehouse was converted into a cinema called Thalia. The site of the birthplace was located somewhere near the stage and the silver screen. The door of the faux-façade served as an emergency exit. The bombardment of May 14, 1940, did the rest. It destroyed the cinema and therefore the last memory of the birthplace of Erasmus. In 2015, a competition was held with the aim of marking the birthplace.

DID YOU KNOW?

## Statue of Erasmus

Around 1620, the famous sculptor Hendrik de Keyser was commissioned to create a bronze statue of Erasmus, who was previously honored with four other statues. The first wooden statue was replaced in 1557 by a statue of blue Belgian limestone (arduin). It was placed in the Grotemarkt (meaning big market), until it was shot to pieces by the Spanish in 1572 and was thrown into a canal. So Erasmus was given a new wooden statue, which was replaced around 1593 by a larger-than-life stone statue. Rotterdam paid dearly for the new bronze statue by De Keyser, which was installed in 1622, again at the Grotemarkt. It was a huge attraction. In 1674, it was brought to the so-called Stadstimmerhuis (the city carpentry) to be repaired, only to be back at the market square in 1677. It survived the Second World War because it had been taken to an underground hiding place in the courtyard of the Museum Boijmans. After the war the statue was first erected again at the Coolsingel, and since 1964 it stands in the square in front of the St. Laurenskerk. On the night of November

21, 1996, it mysteriously fell from its pedestal but didn't suffer any damage. The statue of Erasmus is the first freestanding and the oldest surviving bronze statue in the Netherlands. Copies are in the courtyard of the Erasmus University Rotterdam and on the campus of the Erasmus High School in New York.

## Erasmus:

The most disadvantageous peace is better than the most just war.

**Figure 1.1:** Portrait of Desiderius Erasmus, after a copy by Albrecht Dürer

## Great Church or St. Lawrence Church

Around 1300, the parish of Sint Laurens (St. Lawrence) developed from the 'mother church' in Hillegersberg. The parish church was first mentioned in 1366. Little is known about this church. The construction of the tower of the present Great or St. Lawrence Church began in 1449, near the old parish church. Roughly between 1461 and 1475, the nave was built, for which first the nearby stream – a tributary to the river Rotte – needed to be filled. The entire population was engaged for the act of filling the stream and driving piles. For each pile as many as eighty to hundred men, women and children were needed. On August 10, 1460 – St. Lawrence's Day – the first procession moved from the choir of the old church to the new tower. Five years later, relics of St. Lawrence were placed in the church. Meanwhile, the church was still unfinished. Between 1488 and 1513, the transept and the high choir were built, followed by the north and south chapels, which were completed around 1525. Work on the tower was only restarted after 1547. The Laurenskerk was ready in 1647 when the wooden tower was replaced by a stone elevation.

## The Fire of 1563

Like many cities, Rotterdam had its great fire. The construction of the Grotemarkt (Great Market Square) had only been completed several years when a great fire broke out in the city on July 10, 1563. According to the chronicles of that time it started in a cooperage in the Oostnieuwland (East New Land). In a short time the fire spread to the eastern part of the city. Many houses, herring busses, yards and ship equipment were lost in the fire. The Heilige Geest-Huis (Holy Spirit House), the Hoofdpoort (Main Gate) with the swing bridge over the Kolk, the Oostpoort (East Gate) and the Dominican convent at the Hoogstraat (High Street) were destroyed. As a result of the fire the city's bottlenecks were finally dealt with. The new bridge over the Kolk was constructed further south and on the site of the burned monastery the Pesthuis (Plague House), the Gasthuis (Hospital) and the Dolhuis (Madhouse, Mental Hospital) were built.

# Chapter 2

# First the Revolt, Then the Golden Age (1570-1700)

### *In This Chapter:*

- Rotterdam and Oranje
- City of water and city of land
- Trip around the world
- War ships and merchant ships
- French refugees
- Posh city

For many years the city of Rotterdam and its surroundings were part of the revolt against Spain. The strategic location of the city requires better protection against the Spaniards, resulting in a major urban expansion. The immigrants that came to Rotterdam after the fall of Antwerp in 1585 have much impact on trade, shipping and industry. The commercial network is expanding to the West and East Indies. The economy is flourishing and the population grows. The shipyards move to areas outside the city. The so-called Haringvliet and Boompjes (meaning little trees) become the elite quarter, where chic houses are built. The arrival of Huguenot refugees results in the flourishing of intellectual life in Rotterdam. Around 1700, Rotterdam – with a population of 50,000 souls – is the second city (Amsterdam being the first) in the Republic of the Seven United Provinces (Republiek der Zeven Verenigde Provinciën).

# Rotterdam, City of Oranje

The year 1572 was crucial for Rotterdam. The Spaniards had occupied the Republic. Rotterdam was pro-Spanish, but after the Spanish had killed blacksmith Jan Swart (the first civilian victim) and had caused major damage in the city, the city chose the side of Willem van Oranje (William of Orange). The advantage of this choice was that the city could henceforth participate in the meetings of the States General. From that time the prince would stay in the city on a regular basis. From the city of Rotterdam he led the attack against the Spanish troops. In exchange for substantial, mainly financial, support Rotterdam was allowed to expand the town council, called 'vroedschap'. Moreover, in 1581 Rotterdam was granted the right to vote in the States General. The fact that the remonstrant Johan van Oldenbarnevelt and Hugo de Groot could be appointed as grand pensionary was a result of the tolerant attitude of the city towards religious groups. A majority of the States General were anti-remonstrant, as was Prince Maurits. Since he had to rely on a loyal town council in his fight against the Spaniards, Maurits came to Rotterdam in 1618 to change the law. This meant that the entire town council was dismissed and its number of members reduced and partly renewed.

**Figure 2.1:** On April 9, 1572, the Spanish soldiers committed atrocities after the conquest of Rotterdam

### Marnix van St. Aldegonde

In 1571, nobleman, writer and diplomat Filips van Marnix (1540-1598), Lord of St. Aldegonde, became the assistant to Willem van Oranje. Marnix van St. Aldegonde, as people called him, performed many diplomatic missions. William could also make good use of Marnix's sharp pen for his propaganda in the war against Spain. Moreover, St. Aldegonde managed to decipher encrypted letters of the enemy. In 1573, he was captured during the defense of Rotterdam against the Spaniards. Immediately, Willem van Oranje sent out a message that the prisoner should remain unharmed. If anything happened to him, William would take revenge on the Spaniard Bossu, the governor of the Spanish king in Holland, who had fallen into the hands of Willem's men. Marnix van St. Aldegonde was released one year later after a prisoner exchange. For centuries, St. Aldegonde was believed to be the author of the Wilhelmus, the Dutch national anthem, but these days this opinion is doubted.

## The City Triangle: 1575-1615

Between 1575 and 1615, Rotterdam expanded in the direction of the Nieuwe Maas (New Meuse). This expansion was paid for from the property and funds of the (Catholic) institutions which had been confiscated during the Reformation. In 1575, strategically located Rotterdam, which needed more adequate protection against the Spanish troops, received permission to build fortifications. This had major implications for the development of the city. A new rampart was built parallel to the old one, which turned into an inner harbor as a result. The western part was called Blaak, the eastern part Nieuwehaven (New Harbor). The urban expansion was primarily a military development, but the merchants also saw great benefits for the growing trade and shipping. Starting in 1590, the major port expansion towards the Maas could offer more space to the herring busses and merchant ships. As their names already suggest, the Buizengat (1591) and the Haringvliet (1596) offered space to the fleet of herring busses. In addition, the surroundings of the Haringvliet became a residential and commercial area; the first commodity exchange was built at the Haringvliet/ Spaansekade (Spanish Quay) while the Ooster Oudehoofdpoort (Eastern Old Main Gate) was constructed at the eastern end of the Oudehaven (Old Port). Starting in 1598, a major expansion to the southwest followed, where the Leuvehaven, the Wijnhaven (Wine Harbor) and the Scheepmakershaven (Ship-makers' Harbor) were dug, followed by the Bier (Beer) and Glashaven (Glass Harbor) around 1613. The process was completed in 1614 with the construction of the Boompjes along the quay between the Oudehaven and the Leuvehaven. In their leisure time, the inhabitants of Rotterdam strolled over the promenade along this characteristic riverfront. The construction of the port meant that Rotterdam took over the staple functions of Dordrecht and Middelburg, which turned the city into the main staple market after Amsterdam.

The expansion gave Rotterdam its distinctive triangular shape, enclosed between the Nieuwe Maas in the south, the Goudsevest (vest meaning fortification) in the east and Schiedamsevest and Coolvest in the west. The new expansion area was called Waterstad (Water City) to distinguish it from the old part of town which was called Landstad (Land City). It had large parcels of land where the wealthy built their houses. The expansion process tripled the port area while the urban sectors became twice as large by the addition of Waterstad. Between 1600 and 1700 Rotterdam was one of the fastest growing cities in the Republic.

**Figure 2.2:** Map of Rotterdam, dated to 1632

# The Wide World

In 1585, the Spanish king forbade all trade between the areas he ruled and the Netherlands. Antwerp had always been the staple city for products from Africa, America and Asia entering through Spain and Portugal. After Antwerp had fallen into Spanish hands in 1585, the city no longer functioned as a staple area. With the help of refugee Antwerp merchants such as Johan van der Veeken and Pieter van der Haghe, the Republic itself took action. In 1597, the ship called De Roode Leeuw (The Red Lion) left the port of Rotterdam to trade with overseas territories. After one year she came back from Brazil with a cargo of sugar.

Meanwhile, trading with the East got underway as well, set up by the same Van der Veeken and Van der Haghe. In 1598, they organized a trip through the Strait of Magellan to the East Indies. Five ships from Rotterdam were part of the fleet. The company ended badly. Het Geloof (Faith) was the only ship that returned intact. The other ships fell into the hands of the enemy. Van der Haghe went bankrupt; Van der Veeken survived as he still had plenty of assets in reserve.

DID YOU KNOW?

## Olivier van Noort, first traveler around the world

Olivier van Noort (about 1558-1627) used to exploit the inn called De Dubbele Witte Sleutel (The Double White Key) at the Marktveld (Market Field) in Rotterdam. The adventurous entrepreneur departed from Rotterdam on August 12, 1598, with two ships and two yachts and nearly 250 crew members. The investors were merchants from Rotterdam and Amsterdam. Since the Republic was at war with Spain, the route to India, which had been discovered by the Spaniards, could not be travelled. The aim of this trip was to head to the East Indies via the Strait of Magellan. The trip was not without risk and the crew was at the mercy of scurvy, severe storms and battles with the Portuguese and natives. So it was not surprising that Van Noort returned to Rotterdam with only one ship – the Mauritius – and forty crew members. He arrived on August 26, 1601. In financial terms the trip was a failure because of the loss of several ships and the low yield, namely some pepper and mace. But the Magelhaensche Compagnie (Magellan Company) of Van Noort and his remaining men was the first Dutch company to ever sail around the world.

IMPORTANT

## The first commodity exchange in the Northern Netherlands

The oldest commodity exchange in the Northern Netherlands dates from 1598 and was located in Rotterdam. It was built by the town council. The initiator was the Flemish immigrant Johan van der Veeken (1549-1616). In his time, the merchant, banker and ship-owner was one of the richest men of Rotterdam. The Beurs (Exchange) had three arched galleries which offered shelter to the merchants who concluded their business deals there. Until 1635, the exchange building was located at the corner of the Haringvliet and the Spaansekade. When the English merchants association Fellowship of Merchant Adventures settled in Rotterdam, they demanded a new building. Their demand was met in 1635 when the Exchange took over the building of the former Fish Market at the Blaak. These new premises served as the exchange building until 1720.

## VOC and WIC: East and West

Great rivalry existed between the companies of the merchants who undertook their trading voyages to the East. In 1602, Johan van Oldenbarnevelt, grand pensionary and former town pensionary of Rotterdam, succeeded in putting an end to this by uniting the competitors in the Verenigde Oost-Indische Compagnie (VOC, Dutch East India Company). The VOC was given a monopoly on the voyage to Asia. Amsterdam, Delft, Rotterdam, Hoorn, Enkhuizen and Zeeland were each given a 'room' (a department) in the VOC. The largest gains were made between 1630 and 1650. Especially for the rigging of the VOC ships, the department created a ropery at the Schiedamsevest in 1620. This was a long strip of land where rope was made. Several years later, land and buildings near the Wijnstraat (Wine Street) were purchased in order to meet the demand for warehouse space for the VOC. Until 1632, the ships of the East India Company were built by individuals, until the company established her own wharf at the Scheepmakershaven. That's where the merchant ships were built and equipped.

To be able to make more regular trade trips to Africa and America (including trips for the slave trade), the West-Indische Compagnie (WIC, Dutch West India Company) was founded in 1621. For Rotterdam, the WIC was less successful than the VOC and the initial enthusiasm quickly waned. However, Piet Hein, born in Delfshaven, caused the biggest financial break by capturing a Spanish silver fleet in 1628 in the Bay of Matanzas (Cuba). Another success was the conquest of the Portuguese stronghold of Pernambuco (Recife, Brazil).

DID YOU KNOW?

### Rotterdam donates statue of Piet Hein to Matanzas

On July 27, 1998, Mayor Bram Peper officially donated a statue of Piet Hein to the mayor of Matanzas (Cuba). Piet Hein captured a Spanish silver fleet in 1628 in the Bay of Matanzas. The statue was made by the Rotterdam sculptor Willem Verbon and had been paid for by Rotterdam-based entrepreneur W. van 't Wout. Verbon usually enriched his sculptures with some anecdotal element in order to better characterize the person. In the case of Piet Hein, he left his belt buckle hanging loose. Much to the dismay of Verbon, the beautiful stone pedestal was painted white by the local authorities of Matanzas. It was deemed more appropriate as natural stone is regarded as very common in Matanzas.

## Rivalry with Amsterdam

Until 1650, Amsterdam and Rotterdam each seemed to be going their own way where trade was concerned. Amsterdam focused on the north, Southwest Asia and the East Indies while Rotterdam mainly dealt with Britain, France, Spain, Portugal and the West Indies. But things went wrong when the two cities began to compete. Rotterdam first tried to take from Amsterdam the trade in whale oil and whale bone, which failed. Then they tried to outdo each other by securing the exclusive right of the direct postal communication with England. This was a very important aspect of trade operations as one party could thus delay the letters destined for the competitor. Then there was the failed attempt of Rotterdam to get into the trade in mercury and Westphalian linen and trade goods from Southwest Asia. Although in 1669 a dispute about evasion of import regulations in English woolen sheets was settled with an 'extra-ordinary glass of wine', the competition between Rotterdam and Amsterdam would persist for many centuries.

## Admiralty of the Maze

The Rotterdam Admiralty, also known as the Admiralty of the Maze, is the oldest of the five Dutch admiralties of the Republic. The reason for its foundation was the capture of Brielle by the Sea Beggars in 1572. Supporters of Willem van Oranje united in admiralties for better naval warfare. The first Admiralty College was founded in 1575 in Rotterdam and was led by Willem van Oranje. The college was located at the Botersloot, in the former Sint Agnietenklooster (St. Agnes Convent). In 1644, the Admiralty was given a new building on the corner of Haringvliet/Spaansekade. It got all naval affairs in the province of South Holland under its wing, so it was very powerful. The main tasks of the Admiralty were the construction, equipment, maintenance and manning of warships. In addition, the Admiralty also engaged in the business of protecting the trade at sea, it served as a coast guard, collected due sums of money and took care of implementing the special marine law.

## 's Lands Werf

The powerful Admiralty was an important employer. For the construction of warships the Admiralty built its own shipyard in the city. One of the most famous ships that were constructed on this wharf in 1665 was the Zeven Provinciën (Seven Provinces), the flagship of Michiel de Ruyter. However, as the ships were getting bigger and bigger, new slipways were needed. This was not feasible in the city, where the land was needed for urban expansion. The Admiralty opted for the so-called Reuzeneiland (which – literally translated – means Giant Island or Giant's island but the name probably stems from the family name de Reus) in the Nieuwe Maas. In 1691, the new wharf was inaugurated and named 's Lands Werf, which can be translated as the country's or national wharf. Warships were built there, but not the merchant ships of the Dutch East India Company which had started its own yard in 1685, across the Oostzeedijk.

In 1795, towards the end of the Republic, the Admiralty was dissolved, but the yard continued to exist under the name 's Rijks Werf (State Wharf) or Marinewerf (Naval Wharf) until 1849. The historical site was destroyed in 1940. These days, three apartment buildings are located on the site of the former wharf, and the address is still 's Lands Werf.

## A Place for French Refugees

Several people from Rotterdam bear French names, such as Chabot, Petit and Garnier or 'corruptions' thereof such as Suermondt (Sur Mont) Piekhaar and Pikaar (from Picardy) or Blansjaar (Blanchard). Most likely they are the descendants of refugee French Huguenots.

Under Louis XIV, the Sun King, French Protestants – called Huguenots – were dealt with harshly. In 1685, Louis revoked the Edict of Nantes, which had given the Huguenots greater freedom. This left them without any rights at all. Preachers had the choice to either renounce their faith or leave the country. Protestant schools and churches were destroyed. Hundreds of thousands of Protestants fled the country and left all their possessions behind. Some of them arrived in Rotterdam, such as the theologian and philosopher Pierre Bayle. They were more than welcome because – economically speaking – the country was doing well. The Huguenots automatically received the so-called burgess-ship, meaning citizenship, which was as a rule only granted to those who were born in the city. Normally, foreigners who wanted to start a company should buy citizenship. The Huguenots were generally of better descent and had been well educated. With their fashionable lifestyle they blended in with the rich of Rotterdam, with whom the French language and etiquette were popular. The Huguenots published the French-language newspaper the *Gazette de Rotterdam,* which was also read by the more well-to-do citizens. The Gazette appeared between 1694 and 1716 and is therefore older than the *Rotterdamsche Courant* which first appeared in the year 1717. The city also hoped to benefit from the international contacts of the Huguenots. Two societies were founded for Huguenot women in Rotterdam. These were generally wealthy and enterprising women. They foresaw the need for governesses for the education of the children of the richer middle classes.

After the economic recession of 1688, the tide turned. The privileges of the Huguenots evoked growing protests among the population. The government gradually revoked the privileges and increasingly Huguenots had themselves naturalized. Around 1700, approximately five percent of the population of Rotterdam consisted of former French citizens.

## Chic Buildings in the City

As the city prospered, a number of prestigious buildings were constructed. Among these were three gates on the river side: the Wester and the Ooster Nieuwe Hoofdpoort (the western and eastern new main gates) at the mouth of the Leuvehaven and the Wester Oude Hoofdpoort (the western old main gate) on the west side of the Oudehaven. Also the land side of town was fitted out with new city gates: the Schiedamse Poort and the Oostpoort. The Coolse Poort and the Delftse Poort were restored. The WIC was based in the West Indies House at the Haringvliet and at the end of the seventeenth century the VOC had her new headquarters built at the Boompjes.

The water board of Schieland was also in urgent need of a new home. The Schielandshuis (House of Schieland) was built between 1662 and 1665 by Jacob Lois (ca. 1620-1676) after a design by Pieter Post (1608-1669). This city palace became one of the most striking buildings in the center of town. It was used by the water board until 1840, after which the town council bought it to be converted to a museum. Museum Boijmans was opened in 1849. Tragically, it was largely destroyed by a fire in 1864 which also consumed nearly all the paintings. The museum was rebuilt and is now the only seventeenth-century monument which has survived the bombing of May 14, 1940.

## Neat and clean

In the seventeenth century, Rotterdam was a beautiful and – above all – a clean city. Many a foreigner was amazed by this, such as the French writer and traveler Francois Maximilien Misson, who travelled through Holland in 1687. He thought the city was very clean: 'The houses are kept tidy and clean, both from the outside and from the inside. They're scrubbed and even the wooden facades are thoroughly cleaned from time to time, so that they always appear to be new. The windows always sparkle, as if they were crystal. The streets are so clean that the whole year round women can walk on them wearing their slippers.'

# Chapter 3

# Riots and Renewal; Changing Times (1700-1813)

***In This Chapter:***

- A court painter in Düsseldorf
- The British in Rotterdam
- A remarkable society
- Slave traders
- An Italian architect
- Patriots and Oranje

The prosperity of the Golden Age has definitely ended. The economy is in decline and poverty is on the rise, especially after 1750. Culturally speaking there is a glimmer of light on the horizon as a result of rich society life in Rotterdam. At the end of the century, patriots and royalists are diametrically opposed.

## Adriaan van der Werff: Court Painter in Düsseldorf

Adriaan van der Werff (1659-1722), born in Kralingen as a miller's son, was trained as a painter in Rotterdam by Cornelis Picolet and Eglon van der Neer. In 1676, Van der Werff established himself as an independent painter in Rotterdam. Adriaen Paets, town council member and patron of the arts and sciences, introduced him to the elite. Van der Werff had much success with his portraits and genre pieces, but he nevertheless decided to paint historical pieces and large interior paintings. Paets also ensured that Van der Werff came into contact with the Elector Palatine Johann Wilhelm von der Pfalz in Düsseldorf. And with success. From 1697 to 1716, Van der Werff was his court painter. He thus gained international fame and this not only meant a radical change of his social status, but also of his artistic development. Van der Werff worked only a few months a year for the elector, the remainder of the year he used to live in Rotterdam at the Delftsevaart. In 1703, he was raised to nobility by the elector. Van der Werff was not only a painter, but also an architect. He designed several mansions along the Haringvliet and the Boompjes, as well as the Exchange at the Blaak. All these buildings were destroyed during the 1940 bombing.

### The first Dutch scientific journal

During the seventeenth century all scientific journals appeared in Latin or French. In 1692, the versatile translator and publisher Pieter Rabus published the bimonthly periodical *De Boekzaal van Europa* (The Book Hall of Europe). In this first learned Dutch magazine Rabus showed that the Dutch language lent itself very well to scientific publications. In the successful magazine, Rabus discussed new books and – among other things – described his meetings with the Delft microbiologist Antoni van Leeuwenhoek, who by the way did not know any Latin or other foreign languages. Rabus also talked about current affairs and he stood up for the Rotterdam-based German medical wizard/quack Von Rettwich, who used to heal people from a distance using their urine. Rabus died in 1702.

IMPORTANT

## A new commodity exchange

The Beurs (exchange building, stock market) at the Blaak that had been opened in 1653 had become too small. In 1720, the famous Rotterdam painter Adriaen van der Werff was commissioned by the town council to design a new building. He had his plans ready in 1721, but the actual exchange building was not completed until 1736, long after the death of Van der Werff in 1722. In the nineteenth century the courtyard of the building was fitted out with a cast-iron canopy. The bombing of May 14, 1940, made an end to the Beurs.

# Rotterdam Acknowledges Stadtholder

In 1732, during the Stadtholderless Period (1702-1747), Willem Karel Hendrik Friso visited the shipyard called 's Lands Werf (the admiralty shipyard). Rotterdam's Oranje supporters gave him a warm welcome. This prince of Oranje was made stadtholder in 1747 by the States of Zeeland. He became known as Willem IV, hereditary stadtholder of the Republic, appointed so he could save the country from ruin. Barges from Zeeland bringing the good news to Rotterdam were received by a cheering public. Under pressure from Oranje-minded fellow citizens and for fear of riots in the city, Rotterdam city officials proclaimed Willem IV stadtholder.

Rotterdam was thus the first city in Holland acknowledging him as such. The rest of the country soon followed, which brought an end to the Stadtholderless Period.

## Little London

Already in the seventeenth century, Rotterdam was an interesting city for British merchants. Trading was at a considerable level, especially in manufactured goods, while gin and brandy were exported in return. Most Englishmen lived at the Nieuwehaven (New Harbor) and the Haringvliet. In this area, therefore, the English-Presbyterian and Episcopalian churches were built. During the eighteenth century the British spread across the part of town called Water City, taking up residence at the Blaak, Leuvehaven, Wijnhaven and the posh neighborhood called Boompjes (meaning little trees). This means that the British merchants were well-integrated and that they had a certain social status, since this particular part of town was inhabited by important Rotterdam merchants and regents. So many British merchants came to live in the city for extended periods of time that – in the eighteenth century – Rotterdam was nicknamed 'Little London'. This privileged position came to an end around 1800 as a result of the Napoleonic wars and the Continental System, which brought trade with Britain to a standstill. As they had their own religious communities, the group was able to hold on to its cultural identity for a long time. During the nineteenth century the British managed to connect to the Rotterdam aristocracy.

### An execution in Rotterdam

In 1709, Zacharias Conrad von Uffenbach, from Frankfurt, and his younger brother Johann Friedrich von Uffenbach, made a trip to the Netherlands where they also visited Rotterdam. The two brothers went to the town hall where a couple of executions were imminent. First, several people at the stake were whipped 'in the Dutch way', and then a quack who had stabbed a porter was hanged. The two gentlemen were of the opinion that the most curious aspect of the entire process was that – a few hours before the execution – previously printed tickets were offered for sale with the following text: 'Here are the last words of the beheaded man for the price of an 'oortjen' (a coin, literally the word means little ear).

## Batavian Society for Experimental Philosophy

On June 3, 1769, the Batavian Society for Experimental Philosophy was founded at the initiative of watch and instrument maker Steven Hoogendijk. This society – which still exists today – mainly focused on the practical application of physical science and technology, with the aim of furthering and spreading the knowledge thereof. To this end, the society held competitions – which were published – while lectures were organized, as well as courses (after 1788). During the French period, political and economic tensions rendered the pursuit of science almost impossible. Only in the second half of the nineteenth century the society started flourishing again. The collection of the society, housed in the exchange building (Beurs), was nearly completely lost as a result of the bombing of May 14, 1940.

IMPORTANT

## Steam engines at work

Steven Hoogendijk was particularly interested in water management issues. A steam pumping station for pumping water out of polders and reservoirs was a new phenomenon. Hoogendijk tried to arouse the interest of the city government for constructing a steam engine. While his efforts in 1757 were in vain, in 1774 he achieved better results when the first pumping station in the Netherlands was built at his expense at the Oostpoort (East Gate) in Rotterdam. The steam pumping station was supposed to protect the center of town from excess rainfall and to keep it from flooding. Due to technical shortcomings the efforts remained unsuccessful. In 1787, Hoogendijk had a new pumping station installed – again at his own expense – along the Schie in order to drain the polders Blijdorp and Cool. This time, the steam engine performed successfully. Stadtholder Willem V visited the pumping station, which he admired tremendously. The local population fiercely opposed the pumping station which they called 'Keezending' ('ding' meaning thing, while 'keezen' was the nickname for the innovators who had ordered the building of the station) and as a result the station was demolished in 1791. The foundations were exposed in 2004 by the Office for Archaeological Research Municipal Works Rotterdam (BOOR).

# Theater and Music

Around 1700, the strict church council had banished any form of theater from the city. Theater productions could therefore only be performed at the fair of Delfshaven or in closed communities. As the influence of the church declined around 1750, theater was given more space. There was even a warehouse at the Binnenweg that was rented out to opera and theater entrepreneurs. This enabled the theater company of

Jan Punt from Amsterdam to settle in Rotterdam after the Amsterdam playhouse had been demolished by fire in 1772. A number of Rotterdam entrepreneurs wielded their influence and in 1774 the Rotterdam City Theater was established at the Coolsingel. This theater remained there until 1887, after which a new theater was built in the street called Aert van Nesstraat.

After 1750, concert life also became a more public affair. In a private house at the Bierstraat public concerts were first held in 1756, for which singers were attracted who were on tour. This so-called Groote Concertzaal (Great Concert Hall), the only concert hall in Rotterdam, existed until 1803. After that the owners had the old hall demolished and a 'real' concert hall, designed by architect Jan Giudici, built in its place. The building was destroyed during the bombing of 1940.

DID YOU KNOW?

## An Italian architect in Rotterdam

The Italian-born Carlo Giovanni Francesco (Jan) Giudici (1746-1819) established himself as an architect in Rotterdam in 1770. He realized several buildings in the city such as the Rosaliakerk (1776) in the Leeuwenstraat, the arsenal on the Oostplein (1782) and the Admiralty building in 's Lands Werf (1785). Jan Giudici was appointed in 1786 as an architect and inspector-general of the Admiralty at the Maze and was therefore in charge of all construction and conversion works of the Admiralty. He also designed homes for affluent families along the Leuvehaven, Nieuwehaven, Haringvliet and Boompjes. Giudici not only built in Rotterdam, but also in the surrounding areas. He also developed plans for the city of Assen, which – ultimately – were never realized.

### Merchant houses in Rotterdam

Merchant houses in Rotterdam were of a very different type compared to those in Amsterdam. In Rotterdam the business areas (work and storage spaces) were on the ground floor, and therefore houses had no lifting beams, like in Amsterdam. The residential floors were located directly above one another and there were virtually no cellars and basements. The buildings usually had two entrances: one for the stairs leading to the living areas and one for the business floor. The houses were equipped with high doorsteps and sidewalks.

## Slave Traders Coopstad & Rochussen

The Dutch West India Company (WIC), founded in 1621, was a major player in the slave trade. A kind of trade triangle existed: Dutch goods went to West Africa, where they were traded for slaves. These slaves were then transported to Brazil, North America and the West Indies, where they were sold. Finally the ship would return to the Republic filled with coffee, sugar, tobacco and cocoa. Between 1730 and 1803, after the WIC had suffered financial losses, the slave trade was run by private traders. One of the larger private firms was that of Herman van Coopstad and Isaac Jacobus Rochussen (C & R), both from Rotterdam. Between 1747 and 1777 their company had three ships engaged in a total of 65 slave transports, with an average of almost 310 slaves on board. Some 20,000 slaves in all were transported. The journey from Rotterdam to Liberia, the first port of call, took nearly four months. Usually a ship would then spend seven months sailing along the West African coast in order to exchange firearms, textiles and utensils for slaves, gold and ivory. Elmina Castle in Ghana was usually the last stop to take in slaves.

The journey would then continue to Suriname, or even further to St Eustatius and Curaçao, taking another two months. After a stay of several months, domestic products would be brought back to the homeland. The shareholders invested in a risky project, because a lot could happen during this year-and-a-half. Crop failures, a drop in the price of coffee and cocoa and a major slave uprising in 1773 brought many planters on the edge of a financial abyss. Herman van Coopstad died in 1772. Rochussen continued running the company with Herman Oostendorp, a cousin of Coopstad. Ultimately, the losses outweighed the profits and in 1779 the final curtain fell for Coopstad & Rochussen.

## Oranje Again: Kaat Mossel and Ruige Keet

Catharina (Caatje) Mulder (1723-1798) is better known as Kaat Mossel, owing her nickname to her profession of selling mussels (clams). Like many poor people she was in favor of Oranje since they expected the prince would do much for them. Along with other women such as Keet Zwenke (Rough Kate) and Clasina Verreijn (Orange Lass) from the area called Achterklooster and other lower class neighborhoods, Kaat Mossel stepped to the foreground in 1783 and 1784. They harassed their opponents the Patriots and forced them to wear orange ribbons. This was bound to go wrong and on April 3, 1784, during an attack on the much-hated patriot archer company, someone actually got killed. For their part in the riots Kaat Mossel and Keet Zwenke – much to the delight of the Patriots – were detained in the town hall, receiving a heavy prison sentence. The poet Willem Bilderdijk acted as the lawyer of Kaat Mossel. In 1787, Kaat Mossel, 'stadtholder of the rabble', was acquitted after a preventive detention of more than three years. She became a symbol and Willem Bilderdijk gained national fame.

**Figure 3.1:** Kaat Mossel in the prison located under the town hall of Rotterdam, on Sunday the 28th of November 1784, with the maid and the seamstress of the prison guard

DID YOU KNOW?

## Rumford's soup

Around 1800 there was great distress among the poorest people in Rotterdam. Especially during harsh winters, when heating costs were high, there was little money left over for food. The French occupation had brought trade and shipping to a minimum and the city lived in poverty. The army of beggars increased hand over fist. Every day the poor went through town knocking on the doors of houses asking for alms, causing a lot of inconvenience. Some wealthy citizens founded a so-called Rumford's soup-kitchen in the Stedelijk Lokaal at the Grotekerkplein. Rumford's soup was named after Benjamin Thompson, Count Rumford, who had first tried out his soup in Bavaria. The wealthy citizens of the city bought 'soup cards' and distributed these among the poor, who could then get a bowl of soup four times a week. The first soup distribution took place in the harsh winter of 1800/1801. The soup kitchen was shut down in 1814.

# Napoleon Was Here

Between 1806 and 1810, Louis Napoleon was king of Holland. In 1810, Emperor Napoleon took over and Holland became part of France. He introduced a large number of reforms, such as military service (conscription), civil registration and the metric system. Also, people had to observe mandatory national holidays, such as the anniversary of Napoleon on August 15th and the day of his coronation on the 2nd of December. Accompanied by the continuous shouting of 'Vive l'Empereur' these holidays were celebrated with bells, cannon shots and a parade. At the baptism of Napoleon's son on June 9, 1811, the Boompjes were renamed Quai Napoléon and the Haringvliet became Quai du Roi de Rome, after the honorary title of Napoleon's son.

Rotterdam and the year 1811 are inextricably linked with Emperor Napoleon. Between the 25th and 27th of October, he and his wife Marie Louise visited the city as part of a promotional tour throughout Holland. This short visit cost the city loads of money and those involved had many a sleepless night. The 'Garde d'Honneur' – the obligatory guard of honor – needed to be all dressed up. Rotterdam had to provide lodgings for Napoleon and his extensive entourage. For this purpose the Schielandshuis was chartered and transformed into a hotel. One can imagine the enormous costs involved in this drastic move. Napoleon arrived under harsh weather conditions. He held his audience in the Schielandshuis, visited 's Lands Werf (Admiralty shipyard), made a boat trip and granted the city a new coat of arms enriched with three bees, the symbol of the Bonaparte family.

## Execution of Troublemakers

The regime of Napoleon caused uproar and protest. In April 1813, groups of young men – singing inflammatory songs and shouting 'Oranje Boven' – roamed the streets of towns and villages in the Department Bouches-de-la-Meuse, to which Rotterdam belonged. On April 17, a large crowd disrupted the compulsory registration for the National Guard (military service). The protest quickly spread to the surrounding villages. The French commissioner-general of police, Antoine Delacoux de Marivault, had the suspects of the riot in Rotterdam imprisoned. Three of them were sentenced to death and were shot – on July 7 and 9 – under intense public interest, on the military drill field along the Maas near Schoonderloo.

# Chapter 4

# The Beginning of Modernization (1813-1885)

***In This Chapter:***

- Buried outside the church
- Demolition of the city gates
- Rotterdam and the railway system
- A clean city, a new city
- Riots
- A new waterway
- Rotterdam expands: the leap to South
- Elevated railway track

Until the mid-nineteenth century Rotterdam continues as usual, following the beaten track. It aims for a revival of the old market town. The elite want to expand the transit and staple market, which had been successful in the past. The general conservative atmosphere, also regarding social and cultural issues, prevents economic reforms. After the middle of the century changes are set in motion because the Liberals become politically dominant. The construction of rail links, the digging of the Nieuwe Waterweg (New Waterway) and the development of Feijenoord on the left bank of the Maas (Meuse) are the beginning of modern Rotterdam as a world port.

# Crooswijk General Cemetery

From 1827 onwards, as a result of the French legislation, deceased citizens were no longer allowed to be buried in churches or within the city limits. This was not just to prevent inconvenience by the terrible stench, but served mainly to benefit public health. In 1828, the municipality acquired a parcel of land along the river Rotte. The remains of the homestead Huys Crooswijk, also called Duifhuis (Dove House), were demolished to make way for the construction of a new cemetery. City architect Pieter Adams (1777-1846) designed a plan for this area. The first dead were buried there in July 1832. The entrance was along the Rotte, so that the deceased could also be transported and brought to the cemetery by ship. The entrance gate displayed all sorts of references to death, such as hourglasses, a corpse, inverted torches, bats and crossed scythes. The cemetery was expanded several times and in 1915 the entrance was moved to the Kerkhoflaan (Church Yard Lane or Cemetery Lane). In 1996, Crooswijk General Cemetery became a national monument.

Visit Crooswijk General Cemetery, with its various landscape styles and special burial monuments.

The story goes that sand-bearer Eduard Koning, 41 years old, allegedly said during his work on the new cemetery: ‘I’m wondering who will be the first to be buried here’. According to tradition, it was Koning himself, who died as a result of cholera. In that year the cholera took 700 lives. Eduard Koning, born in Overschie, died on July 20, 1832, aged 41 years, seven months and seven days.

# The City Gates Disappear

Rapidly growing Rotterdam was bursting at the seams. Rotterdam had some 90,000 inhabitants, who lived for the most part in the overcrowded city. The surrounding walls and city gates impeded expansion of the city. When defensive walls were no longer needed, it was a good opportunity to break them down. Between 1827 and 1856, eight of the ten gates ('poort' in Dutch) fell victim to the demolition hammers. The first was the Schiedamsepoort in 1827. The Wester Oude Hoofdpoort at the Oudehaven followed in 1828. The Ooster Oude Hoofdpoort on the other side of the Oudehaven succumbed in 1856. It had to give way to a station of the Rhijnspoorweg-Maatschappij (Rhine Railway Company). The residents at the Haringvliet protested because their view would be obstructed. Nevertheless, the gate was demolished, but not for the new station, which was eventually constructed as the Maasstation in 1876 at the Oosterkade. In 1832 and 1854, the Ooster Nieuwe Hoofdpoort and the Wester Nieuwe Hoofdpoort on both sides of the Leuvehaven also fell victim to demolition. The Hofpoort at the Weena (the gate that was the last to be build, in 1788) stood in the way when – in 1831 – the water between the Rotte and the Schie was filled and the land subsequently used for the fair and the cattle market. When the Coolse Poort and the Goudse Poort were also taken down, only the Oostpoort and the Delftse Poort survived the nineteenth century.

DID YOU KNOW?

## First gasworks

In 1825, Sir William Congreve bought a piece of land along the Zalmhaven (Salmon Harbor). With the approval of the municipality he founded the first coal-gas factory of the Netherlands, the Imperial Continental Gas Association (ICGA). It delivered gas to individual people for lighting their homes and later to the municipality for street lighting. In 1852, a few private entrepreneurs founded the Nieuwe Rotterdamsche Gasfabriek (New Rotterdam Gasworks) at the Oostzeedijk in Kralingen, which was responsible for the lighting of public buildings. After the municipality had founded its own gasworks in 1876, private gas production was brought to an end during the eighties.

## Rowing and Sailing in Rotterdam

Aquatic sports have been a tradition in Rotterdam since 1845. In that year the Koninklijke Nederlandsche Yachtclub (Royal Dutch Yacht Club) was founded, a water sports club for the Rotterdam elite. Prince Hendrik was its president. The club had its home at the Willemskade, where the clubhouse had been built by the Amsterdam architect A.N. Godefroy. From the balcony, the shipping magnates and other dignitaries were able to watch the matches on the water. The yacht club did not fare well and Prince Hendrik had to come to its financial rescue on a regular basis. His death in 1879 also meant the death of the club; the final curtain fell in 1882. Its large collection of ship models and ethnological objects form the basis of the current Maritiem Museum Rotterdam and the Wereldmuseum (World Museum), which is still located in the original clubhouse.

The still existing Roei- en Zeilvereniging De Maas (the rowing and sailing club) was founded in 1851. The club was very successful and even had 150 members at the very start, including Prince Hendrik. Like the yacht club, it was only open to affluent citizens. Its home was situated at the Veerhaven. In 1884, the expansion of the harbor forced the club to move to the Katendrechtse Veer, to return again to the Veerhaven for the same reason in 1908. There they had a new clubhouse built, designed by the Rotterdam architects Barend Hooijkaas jr. and Michiel Brinkman.

## The Railroad in Rotterdam

The first railway in Rotterdam dates from 1847 and was operated by the Hollandsche IJzeren Spoorweg-Maatschappij (HIJSM, Holland Iron Railway Company). The railway was the connection between Amsterdam and Rotterdam. The terminal station was situated at the Delftse Poort, the main station of the HIJSM. However, there was no good connection to the south. The train from Antwerp only went as far as Moerdijk at Hollands Diep. The passengers had to transfer to a ferry that took them to Rotterdam. A horse omnibus transported passengers from the dock to the Delftse Poort station. From there one could continue the trip.

In 1855, a second rail link was constructed in Rotterdam: the connection to the Rhijnspoorweg to Utrecht. Since 1843, the big competitor Antwerp had a direct connection to Cologne. It became all too clear to Rotterdam that it was vital to create a similar connection. The trains of the Rhijnspoorweg Company started their journey from a makeshift station. Only with the construction of the Maas station in 1876, the railway company was given a proper station. In 1877, station Beurs (Exchange) was added as part of the elevated railway. These three stations, which were owned by different railway companies, lacked a true connection, so the passengers had to be transported between the stations by horse tram.

## Coolsingel Hospital

Willem Nicolaas Rose (1801-1877), who came to work for the city of Rotterdam as an urban architect in 1839, designed the Coolsingel Hospital. It replaced the very outdated Stedelijk Gasthuis (Municipal Hospital) at the Hoogstraat (High Street). The draft was approved by the municipality in 1840, but as the construction costs proved to be much higher than budgeted, the hospital was only completed in 1851. But then it was certainly one of the most modern in the country. Together with medical director J.B. Molewater, Rose had created a hospital for which even foreigners came to Rotterdam. Also the clinical education now took place in the hospital. During the bombing of May 14, 1940, the Coolsingel Hospital was heavily damaged. In 1961, it was replaced by the Gemeenteziekenhuis (Municipal Hospital), from 1967 called Academisch Ziekenhuis Dijkzigt (Academic Hospital Dijkzigt).

## Clean City: the Water Project

Willem Nicolaas Rose did not only design the Coolsingel Hospital, he worked on many other projects. He became very well-known because of the Water Project. One of his initial ideas was to address the outdated water management. Dirty water had caused the cholera epidemic of 1832. To refresh the water in the city, Rotterdam used the flow of the tides of the river Maas. But only the part of town called Waterstad (Water City), situated on the other side of the embankment, could benefit from this system. To be able to get clean water into the center of town and the dirty water out, Rose came up with a sewage plan in 1842. Due to a difference in height, clean water from the Maas could be stored in the city defense canals, and from there on it was led to the polluted ditches. Rose designed a system of canals surrounding the city for the drainage of the non-built-up area. These canals were in fact the new border between the city and the countryside. Initially, the plan was rejected by the municipality, but after another cholera epidemic the town-council reluctantly gave permission for the plan in 1854, albeit in a reduced form. By constructing public garden strips along the canals the project also contributed to a more beautiful city. The Water Project was completed in 1862.

IMPORTANT

### Merchant in pigments and paint

The Rotterdam merchant Henricus Franciscus Caroluszoon (Hendrik) Tollens (1780-1856) was not only active as a paint dealer. He was best known for his many poems. In his time he was considered the greatest poet of the Netherlands. Until 1932 his composition 'Wien Neerlandsch Bloed' was the Dutch national anthem. In 1932, Queen Wilhelmina established the Wilhelmus as the national anthem. Tollens died in Rijswijk. To honor his memory a statue was called for. A national committee was therefore set up, hosting people from Rotterdam, Amsterdam and The Hague. Still, the money needed for the statue could only be raised with great difficulty. And then the choice of an appropriate place was fought over. On September 24, 1860, four years after the death of Tollens, the marble statue, designed by the sculptor Johann Theodor Stracké, was solemnly unveiled in Het Park. This happened in the presence of King Willem III and the princes Willem and Frederik, several ministers, the royal governor and the entire town council. Unfortunately the marble could not resist the harsh Dutch winter weather and therefore every fall the municipality placed a large wooden case over the statue. In the spring, usually a week before Easter, Tollens would come out again. This lasted until 1960, when the statue was impregnated in order to survive the winter.

## Jacob de Vletter: Hero or Victim?

The Rotterdam activist Jacob de Vletter (1818-1872) fought for better conditions of the people. Coming from humble origins himself, he managed to climb the social ladder and work as a teacher. He was appointed director of a school for poor children, but was dismissed again because of a conflict with its board members. In 1866, he became editor at the *Rotterdamsch Weekblad* (Rotterdam Weekly Newspaper). He used the newspaper to express his displeasure with the municipal authorities and the police. This made him rather unpopular, but his writings were not a danger to the social order.

Soon the newspaper flooded with complaints about the middle class and the town council that was supposedly paying more attention to the expansion of the port than to issues like health care, housing and public facilities. De Vletter's articles gave the newspaper a bad name and he was fired. In the hot summer of 1868, De Vletter called on people to take a refreshing plunge in the city canals. He was thus actually reviving an ancient custom: on hot days, poor residents used to go swimming in open water outside the urban districts. But since the Water Project designed by Rose, the clean water in the canals was of course more attractive. Because of his provocation De Vletter was arrested but soon released again, which further increased the anxiety among the people. In the evening of October 31, riots broke out. Because the police were nowhere to be seen, thousands of people gathered at the police station near the town hall. A real battle ensued, with attempted arson in the town hall and the police station. Policemen saw no other way out but fleeing to the roof. Eventually, after some further disturbances, calm returned to the city. The next morning, army troops that had been called in for assistance restored power and arrested De Vletter in his house. He was sentenced to ten years imprisonment. The public outcry over this harsh sentence was big. During his trial, De Vletter asked the help of Multatuli, who was convinced of his innocence and who visited him in prison. In an open letter to members of parliament he pleaded for clemency. In the end, De Vletter's sentence was reduced and he was released early March 1872. However, by then he was so weak that he died a few months later.

## Nieuwe Waterweg

As a result of the silting-up of the river Maas, merchant ships had to make an increasingly large detour to get into Rotterdam. This was very inefficient, especially because for the industrialized nations England and Germany it was becoming ever more important that raw materials and products reached their destination – via Rotterdam – as quickly as possible. Rotterdam therefore needed a rapid transit system to be able to compete with other countries. In 1857, the specialist in water management Pieter Caland (1826-1902) came up with a bold plan to build a canal through the dunes near Hoek van Holland. It had to be an open connection to the sea without locks. The plan was approved in 1863 and its implementation started in 1866. In 1872, the first merchant ship entered the Nieuwe Waterweg (New Waterway), but the problems proved to be far from over. The tidal action was not sufficient to keep the depth of the canal at the necessary level. Dredgers offered the solution, but the Nieuwe Waterweg did not reach the required depth until 1885. From then on, Rotterdam was able to develop into a world port. Because of the constant need for dredging, construction was considerably more expensive than budgeted. For Caland, exceeding the budget was a reason to submit his resignation.

# A Leap over the River

## Connecting the river banks

The Nieuwe Waterweg resulted in new port activities. In the overcrowded city triangle there was no room for any more activities so Rotterdam was forced to move to the other side of the Nieuwe Maas. The expansion was also necessary for the construction of the Zuider-Staatsspoorweg (Southern State Railway). The first area to be annexed (in 1869) was the island Feijenoord, on the left bank of the Maas, which belonged to the municipality of IJsselmonde.

At the time, Feijenoord was still virtually uninhabited, with the exception of the former infirmary to which G.M. Roentgen had transferred his company the Rijnstoomsleepvaart (steam tug boats on the river Rijn). Also the territories – along the Maas – of the autonomous municipality Charlois were added to the city, as well as Katendrecht (part of the Charlois municipality). This called for new river crossings: across the Maas as a connection between the city and the Noordereiland (Northern Island) and across the Noorderhaven (Northern Harbor) as a connection between the Noordereiland and Feijenoord.

The Northern Island had been created by digging the Noorderhaven. In 1874, during a visit of King Willem

III, the name was changed from Noorderhaven to Koningshaven (King's Harbor). The permanent railway bridge over the Maas was completed in 1877, and so was the railway swing bridge (movable bridge) over the Koningshaven. The swing bridge had been especially made for large ships that couldn't pass under the fixed railway bridge. In 1927, the swing bridge was replaced by a railroad lift bridge, soon called 'De Hef' ('heffen' means to lift). In 1878, the Willemsbrug was built next to the railway bridge over the Maas. This particular bridge was meant for the other traffic. Then in 1880 the second crossing over the Koningshaven was finished: the Koninginnebrug (Queen's Bridge). This allowed factories to settle in the eastern area, such as brewery d'Oranjeboom in 1885 and the margarine industry Van den Bergh in 1891. Rotterdam thus became a transit port, but very soon the harbor complex at Feijenoord, with its narrow approach ports, became too small. Rotterdam was ready for a new expansion.

## Pincoffs or: the Big Scandal

Thanks to the Rotterdamsche Handelsvereeniging (RHV, Rotterdam Trade Association) Feijenoord could develop on the left bank of the Maas. In 1872, Lodewijk Pincoffs founded the RHV with a capital of 15 million guilders, at that time an unprecedented sum. Many top members of the Rotterdam financial world, including the famous Marten Mees, took part in the RHV. Around 1880 – with more than 30 million in investment funds from the RHV, the city and the government – Rotterdam had several ports, yards and streets at its disposal on the island of Feijenoord. The RVH also developed the Binnenhaven (Inner Harbor) and the Entrepothaven, ports that were very suitable for the transshipment of non-bulk cargo. During this period the Entrepot-building – meant for storage – as well as the Poortgebouw (Gatehouse) were built, the latter serving as the headquarters of the RHV. In 1879, when it was discovered that Pincoffs had used

RHV-money to keep his African Trade Association alive – which failed by the way – the RHV collapsed. Pincoffs fled to America and left the RHV with a debt of over a million. For a long time he was vilified, but finally his importance as an innovative entrepreneur to develop Rotterdam was decisive. And so it was decided on October 23, 1992, to name a road, a square and a bridge after him. They are all located on the so-called Kop van Zuid. Furthermore, in front of the Entrepot-building there is a statue of Pincoffs, and late 2007 a Hotel Pincoffs was opened at the Stieltjesstraat.

## Railway Overpass across the City

During the last quarter of the nineteenth century, the city of Rotterdam changed a great deal. In 1871, a major traffic breakthrough took place near the Binnenrotte, originally a part of the river Rotte. High above the city an overpass was built with a rail link. Passing across the city, the 2.2 km-long overhead railway connected the Beurs station and the railway bridge over the river Maas. It was the only railway in the Netherlands running through a historic city center. The railway was part of the connection Amsterdam-Breda. The opening of the Binnenrotte-overpass took place on April 28, 1877. For the purpose of building the overpass the Binnenrotte had been filled up in 1871, thus finally bringing an end to that part of the Rotte along which Rotterdam came into being. The breakthrough required the demolition of many houses, including a row of townhouses along the Wijnhaven, but also the Korenbeurs (Corn Exchange) at the Steiger. The air track cut the old city center in two for over a hundred years, until it was demolished in 1993 after it had been made redundant by the construction of the Willemsspoortunnel.

## Hal and Lloyd

Rotterdam used to have two major carriers: Koninklijke Lloyd (Royal Lloyd) and the Holland-Amerika Lijn (HAL). As a passenger carrier HAL is the oldest. Rotterdam Lloyd is inextricably linked to the Ruys family. In 1839, Jan Willem Ruys Daniëlszoon (1809-1889) laid the foundation for a regular service between the Netherlands and the Dutch East Indies with the barque (a special type of sailing vessel) called Cornelis Wernard Eduard. His ships transported mainly freight. In 1875, the company carried the name Stoomboot-Reederij Rotterdamsche Lloyd. As the firm consisted of several independent smaller companies, it was decided in 1893 to establish one single company: the NV Stoomvaart Maatschappij Rotterdamsche Lloyd, popularly known as 'Lloyd'. In collaboration with the Stoomvaart Maatschappij Nederland in Amsterdam, weekly steamboat services to the East could take place, starting in 1887. There was a separate and fast service for carrying passengers and mail, and another service for the transport of freight.

In 1870, the HAL started its life – with money from Marten Mees and Lodewijk Pincoffs – as a partnership company of Antoine Plate and Otto Reuchlin. Their goal was to maintain a direct link with America by steamship. Their first journey took place in 1872. In 1873, when Plate, Reuchlin & Co had two ships, the company was transformed into the Nederlandsch-Amerikaansche Stoomvaart Maatschappij (NASM), operating a fleet of ships with names like Statendam, Nieuw Amsterdam and Rotterdam. With the construction of the Nieuwe Waterweg, which was open for large steamships from 1875, New York became a regular destination. As people mainly used the name Holland-Amerika Lijn, this name was added to the NSAM in 1896. In daily practice, the company was referred to as HAL. In 1989, HAL was acquired by the American Carnival Corporation & plc. Lloyd had lost its independent existence in 1970 when all scheduled services were brought together in the Koninklijke Nedlloyd Groep.

# Plan C

With its many bridges and roads, Rotterdam was a cluttered city. Especially at the intersection Blaak, Oudehaven, Kolk and Kleine Draaisteeg traffic used to get stuck. Director of Public Works G.J. de Jongh (1845-1917) designed some plans to improve traffic flow. Plan C was an impressive urban intervention between the Kolk and the Oudehaven (Old Port). Parts of the Kolk and the Old Port were filled and provided with vaults so as not to impede inland navigation. Simultaneously, the vaulted overpass provided more space for roads. Plan C was built on the newly created area. On the ground floor shops were located. Arcades were built on the side of the Oudehaven and the Kolk, allowing shoppers to stay dry when it rained and to walk in the cool shade when it was hot. The two upper floors contained offices and homes. Below Plan C two passage ways were constructed for navigation between the Kolk and the Old Port. Until May 1940, Plan C was a popular place for shopping.

## Chapter 5

# Major Port City (1885-1914)

### *In This Chapter:*

- A second expansion phase
- Villages and polders disappear
- Waves of immigrants
- Annexations
- Emancipation
- Traffic breakthrough

By the time it is clear that Rotterdam needs to let go of old ideas about the staple market, subsequently embracing the transit trade, this has far-reaching consequences. The old town harbors are too small for the ever larger ships. Even the recently built port complex at Feijenoord with its narrow harbor basins no longer suffices. To enable the transshipment of bulk cargo on a large scale, new docks will need to be constructed. The only place where this is possible once again proves to be the left bank of the Maas. Villages and polders will have to make way for the new harbors. The new industries attract many laborers. The rapid urban development not only creates an entirely new cityscape, it also leads to political and social unrest.

# The Expansion Phase

The urge to create a larger harbor leads to the annexation of surrounding areas and communities, both on the left and on the right bank of the river Maas.

## Left bank of the Maas

In 1869, Feijenoord in IJsselmonde had been the first annexation on the left bank of the river Maas, but soon the narrow ports were no longer adequate. New ports were built under the guidance of G.J. de Jongh, Director of Public Works since 1879 and the successor to W.N. Rose. De Jongh took his inspiration for the new port designs from the Maas itself, having the idea to create large basins. These were immense ports in themselves, easily accessible for seagoing vessels. Henceforth, ships were no longer required to pass annoying bridges, as was the case with the narrow canal ports, but they could easily enter the harbor. This allowed Rotterdam to develop as a transit port for the German hinterland.

## Harbors at the left bank of the Maas

KEY MOMENT

The Rijnhaven (1887-1893) was the first harbor that was dug under the direction of De Jongh. After that the Eerste (first) Katendrechtse Haven followed in 1893, the Tweede (second) Katendrechtse Haven between 1895 and 1896 and finally the Maashaven (1898-1905). The Maashaven was twice as large as the Rijnhaven and was realized in the territory of Charlois, which was annexed in 1895. For this purpose the old village of Katendrecht had to be demolished. Not only the simple working-class houses were lost, but also the beautiful, large country houses of the wealthy families of Rotterdam. North of the Maashaven the new working-class quarter Katendrecht was built. Both the Rijnhaven and the Maashaven were huge projects, but they were insignificant compared to the Waalhaven (1906-1931). This harbor of over three hundred hectares was constructed in three phases. It could accommodate 140 vessels. On the northeast side was the harbor inlet, which gave access to the petroleum complexes along the Sluisjesdijk in the rapidly industrializing Charlois. Northwest of the Waalhaven was the complex of the Rotterdamsche Droogdok Maatschappij (RDM, Rotterdam Dry-dock Company), one of the major shipyards in the area of the Nieuwe Waterweg.

The ports on the left bank of the Maas were intended for the transshipment of bulk goods. Transshipment of non-bulk cargo took place on the right bank.

**Figure 5.1:** Loading coal while still in the middle of the river; harbor works on the Nieuwe Maas in 1930

## *Right bank of the Maas*

During the eighties of the nineteenth century, a serious shortage of loading bays had arisen on the right bank of the river Maas. The old harbors in the city had become less and less accessible for the ever growing ships. During the directorship of De Jongh, the Parkhaven (1890-1893), Schiehaven (1904-1909) and Sint-Jobshaven (1906-1908) were constructed. Delfshaven was annexed by Rotterdam in 1886, at its own request. De Jongh developed an expansion plan for the Coolpolder, which was only realized after the construction of the port railway in 1903. The possibilities for the construction of new non-cargo ports depended on the willingness of Schiedam to cede territory. Between 1912 and 1916, after part of Schiedam had been added to Rotterdam, the so-called Vierhavenplan (four harbor plan) could be realized, consisting of the construction of the Koushaven, the IJsselhaven, the Lekhaven and the Keilehaven.

DID YOU KNOW?

### Sludge for park and forest

Public Works Director G.J. de Jongh had the idea to use the excess soil resulting from digging the harbors for raising other locations elsewhere in Rotterdam. In 1896, with sludge from the Tweede Katendrechtse Haven, a hill was created in The Park. That particular section of The Park – located outside the embankment – was thus protected against the water. The so-called 'Bult van De Jongh' (De Jongh's Hump) still offers a magnificent view over the river. The sand from the Waalhaven was used for raising the area near the Kralingse Plas (Lake Kralingen). This was the beginning of the Kralingse Bos (Kralingen Forest), which turned Kralingen into a recreational area.

# Waves of Immigration

Throughout the centuries, many immigrants settled in the city.

## Farmers

After 1880, employment in the new transit ports and related industries attracted many migrants from the province. Between 1890 and 1910, the population grew from about 210,000 to 430,000 souls. The largest group came from

Zuid-Holland, followed by people from Noord-Holland, Gelderland, Zeeland and West-Brabant. Most of them settled across the Meuse in the area simply called Zuid (South). Many of the 'original' inhabitants of Rotterdam regarded the newcomers as peasants. The actual farm workers from Zeeland and West-Brabant contributed a great deal to that perception. Zuid was therefore also called the 'Boerenzij', the peasants' side.

The city expanded to the borders of neighboring municipalities, which did the same in the opposite direction. Rotterdam and Delfshaven therefore slowly grew together, which gave Rotterdam a reason for annexing Delfshaven – at its own request – in 1886. The development of the city was necessary to meet the demand for cheap working-class houses. The newcomers found themselves in various professions. Many found work as a day laborer at the harbor. In 1889, due to the large concentration of workers in the port, the first big strike broke out, ending in a victory for the workers.

## *Emigrants*

Another group of temporary immigrants consisted of the East European Jews who fled their countries between 1880 and 1914 due to growing anti-Semitism. This wave of political refugees largely passed by the Netherlands, but Rotterdam got its share. From the city on the Maas, tens of thousands of people crossed the ocean to the New World with the Nederlandsch-Amerikaansche Stoomvaart-Maatschappij (Dutch-American Steamship Company) later called HAL. In 1893 alone, almost 36,000 emigrants left the European continent through Rotterdam. For the purpose of housing these refugees, the NASM opened a hotel at the Wilhelminakade in 1893. A large part of the refugees arrived in Rotterdam in appalling conditions. In 1883, the Jewish community set up the Vereniging Montefiore (Society Montefiore) for them, to provide relief and shelter to the passing refugees.

The Wilhelminakade houses the former offices of the Holland-America Line. In 1993, the building was transformed into the Hotel New York, where you can still taste the atmosphere of the old HAL.

## *Chinese*

In the early twentieth century, the Chinese formed a group of migrants that played a major role in the Rotterdam shipping industry. In 1911, Rotterdam ship owners brought Chinese sailors to our country to break a harbor strike. That was the beginning of the Chinese community in Rotterdam. Ships that did not regularly pull into any of the Rotterdam ports would moor in Katendrecht. The sailors were dependent on Chinese shipping masters, a kind of subcontractors who negotiated with shipping companies and provided shelter. Katendrecht, which was already known as an entertainment area with an international audience of mostly sailors, became a typical sailors' district with its own China Town.

### The Passage

Not everyone knows that Rotterdam once had a wonderful Passage (mall), which was even the first of the Netherlands. In 1877, the company M. Hakkert Comp reported to the mayor and council that they had acquired several houses with their associated stables and gardens at the Korte Hoogstraat, with the intention of building a glass-covered street. This street – consisting of houses and shops – would connect the Hoogstraat to the Coolvest. On October 15, 1879, the 100-meter long Passage, designed by the architect J.C. van Wijk, was opened by the mayor. It was built exactly on the pedestrian route between the Hoogstraat – at the time the main shopping street of Rotterdam – and the Binnenweg. The Passage had two levels. The side of the Coolvest was more than 2.80 meters lower than the Korte Hoogstraat, which then served as a water barrier. Because of the difference in elevation, there was a separate downstairs passage, but because hardly anyone used it ultimately it was turned into a municipal swimming pool. The Passage, which was about 20 meters high, had nearly 20 stores with above it some 70 homes. In 1881, experiments with electric light were carried out there and in 1883 the Nederlandsche Electriciteitsmaatschappij (Dutch Electricity Company) provided electricity, for the first time through a cable, from its electricity plant at the Baan. Especially Café du Passage, where as many as 172 light bulbs were installed, attracted much attention. The Passage existed until May 1940.

## Van Beuningen and Boijmans

Museum Boijmans owes part of its collection to Daniël George van Beuningen (1877-1955), who became director of the Rotterdam branch of the Steenkolen Handels Vereeniging (SHV, Coal Traders Association) in 1902. He made sure that SHV became the leading company in the fields of transportation, storage and trading of coal from the German Ruhr area. Van Beuningen was the owner of a shipyard and a boat-towing service. He also established the harbor taxi company Spido, as well as a sea shipping company. He was involved in the founding of the Havenziekenhuis (Harbor Hospital) and the construction of the Feyenoord Stadium. By means of his coal-earned money Van Beuningen acquired a very important art collection. Most of the works of art ended up in Museum Boijmans, which added Van Beuningen to its name in 1958.

## Annexation of Kralingen and Hoek van Holland

Kralingen consisted of a narrow strip of land between the peat lakes that came into being as a result of centuries of cutting peat. The strong population growth in the city made the wealthy citizens move to the rural area of Kralingen. The Kralingen municipality took the initiative to be annexed by Rotterdam, which happened in 1895. Kralingen was not important for the expansion of the ports, which made it the perfect place for the wealthy citizens of Rotterdam. So the lakes were drained, except for the Kralingse Plas, and the soil was made suitable for building upon.

Hoek van Holland was a different case as it belonged to the municipalities of 's-Gravenzande and Naaldwijk. In this virtually uninhabited region a community had grown (in 1863) of men who had been hired for the construction of the Nieuwe Waterweg (New Waterway). They lived there under primitive conditions in makeshift housing and with poor infrastructure and inadequate sanitation. When the Nieuwe Waterweg was completed in 1872, the railroad was extended. For the passengers, the Nieuwe Waterweg and the railway from Hoek van Holland to Rotterdam were very important for a fast shipping connection. The maiden voyage of the ferry Hoek van Holland-Harwich took place on the first of June, 1893. That year also witnessed the opening of the railway Hoek van Holland-Maassluis. The penniless Hoek van Holland was added to Rotterdam on January 1, 1914.

### First birth after the annexation

According to the annexation laws a mayor was allowed to appoint a special officer with the implementation of the law, administrative regulations and ordinances. Since the distance between Hoek van Holland and Rotterdam was too big, Cornelis François Jas (1875-1968) was appointed Commissioner on January 1, 1914, in Hoek van Holland, under the direct responsibility of the mayor of Rotterdam, but with a high degree of independence. He was also head of the local municipal and state police, official of the civil registry and warden of stray finds at the beach. Hoek van Holland got an auxiliary administrative office for records of births and marriages. The first birth after the annexation was on January 7, 1914. The child Cornelis Korteland, son of W.C. Korteland and A.P. van der Gaag, received from the municipality of Rotterdam a post office savings bank book with 10 guilders.

# Emancipation

## Workers and women

Two individuals in particular made a case for the emancipation of workers and women: Hendrik Spiekman (1874-1917) and Suze Groeneweg (1875-1940). Journalist and social counselor Spiekman was one of the founders of the Sociaal-Democratische Arbeiderspartij (SDAP, Social Democratic Workers' Party). In 1901, he founded the Bestuurdersbond (association of officials) of which many socialist associations and institutions became members, such as the SDAP. Spiekman tried to organize the Rotterdam port workers by establishing the Algemene Havenarbeidersvereniging (General Dock Workers' Association) in 1902. In this way he wanted to foster solidarity and thus realize organized harbor protests. In 1901, Spiekman had become the first SDAP councilman in Rotterdam, and thus the first socialist in the town council. He made a strong case for social improvements and a good municipal housing policy. He started an Office for Labor Law, where – for many years – he advised organized and non-organized workers. Spiekman became a member of the elected council of the provinces for Zuid-Holland and of the Dutch parliament. His death in 1917 came as a big shock to his followers and his burial ceremony attracted much popular attention.

Suze Groeneweg was a teacher in Dordrecht and Rotterdam and as such an ardent advocate for public education. She joined the SDAP in 1903. She became a member of its Departmental Board and in 1908 also of the Federation Board. Within the Rotterdam department of the SDAP she founded a women's propaganda club in 1905. However, she was not after the foundation of separate women's organizations, but thought that men and women within the party should treat each other on a basis of equality. In 1918, she became the first woman elected by the SDAP as a member of parliament and a year later as a member of the Rotterdam city council. She was a pacifist and within parliament she was mainly engaged in matters of education, the fight against excessive use of alcohol (temperance), infant and maternity care and disarmament. She also advocated a statutory leave of absence during pregnancy and childbirth.

## Rascals

Initiatives for improving the lot of poor and ragged children came from people within the educational system. Socially motivated teachers who taught in poor neighborhoods wanted to change something about the miserable condition of these children. In 1884, August Pieter van Groeningen (1866-1894) was appointed as a teacher at the so-called Kosteloze School (cost-free school) at the Boezemstraat. In tough unpolished language he published about the harsh lives of children and adults in the working-class neighborhoods. Also Henri Hartog (1869-1904), a teacher born in Schiedam, wrote a lot about abuses. He stood at the cradle of the association Voor de kunst (For the Arts) which aimed to bring the workers into contact with art. Hartog wrote the text of the song *Het broekje van Jantje* (Jantje's pants, sung by Koos Speenhoff and later by Mary Servaes who used the artists' name Zangeres zonder Naam, singer without a name).

Some teachers actually went into the poor neighborhoods to see the misery with their own eyes. Teacher and journalist Louis Schotting (1870-1957) visited the slums together with Hendrik Spiekman. They visited as many as 860 homes of the poor, limiting themselves to the buildings that were accessible through passageways and alleys. The number of slum dwellings in Rotterdam was in fact much higher. They were shocked by the horrible circumstances: unemployment, abusive yelling and shouting, fights, drunkenness, disease and crime. In order to wake up those in society who were better-off they wrote down their experiences, published under the title *Arm Rotterdam. Hoe het woont! Hoe het leeft!* (which can be roughly translated as The poor of Rotterdam. What their houses are like and how they live!)

About the same time, Chris van Abkoude (1880-1960) also visited 'darkest' Rotterdam, as he called it. He was a teacher at a public school in Rotterdam. What he came across was beyond his imagination. Thousands of children were starving, which he could only believe when he saw it with his own eyes. The neighborhood of the Zandstraat was an actual hell. According to Van Abkoude even the animals in the zoo were better looked after and had cleaner places to stay than the people living in the Zandstraat quarter. Van Abkoude wrote a series of articles on the subject in the newspaper Dagblad van Rotterdam. In 1904, his sketches were gathered in a brochure called *Droevig leven in Rotterdam. Een onderzoek naar den toestand van behoeftige schoolkinderen.* (Miserable lives in Rotterdam; An investigation into the condition of needy schoolchildren). To present the reader with some kind of image of the conditions he described, the booklet was provided with photographs by amateur photographer Adriaan Brouwer. Van Abkoude was also the author of *Pietje Bell, of de lotgevallen van een ondeugenden jongen* (Pietje Bell, or the adventures of a little rascal), published in 1914.

## Boefje

One of the first children's books with the 'deprived' child as a subject was *Boefje* (rascal) in 1903. The writer and socialist Marie Joseph Brusse was the author. In 1901, Brusse had been granted custody of Jantje Govers by the foundation called Pro Juventute, which campaigned for the disadvantaged child. Jantje was rude, untidy and neglected, but his heart was in the right place. Brusse knew more of such 'rascals'. Experiences with his foster child, who – along with his friend Pietje Puk – used to muck about in the port of Rotterdam and raise hell every now and then, appeared as a serial in the *Nieuwe Rotterdamsche Courant.* The stories were published as a book and then reworked into a play and performed hundreds of times, with a special rendition by actress Annie van Ees. On March 14, 1980, a statue of Boefje, made by the artist Tineke Slingerland, was unveiled by Mayor André van der Louw at Amman Square in Rotterdam.

## First Nobel Laureate in Chemistry

In 1901, the physical chemist Jacobus Henricus van 't Hoff (1852-1911) was the first Nobel Laureate in Chemistry. He is considered one of the founders of stereochemistry and physical chemistry. Van 't Hoff was born in Rotterdam and attended Secondary School there (Hogere Burgerschool, HBS). He studied chemistry in Delft, Leiden, Bonn, Utrecht and Paris and finally graduated in Utrecht. In 1878, he became a professor in Amsterdam and then in 1896 in Berlin. Shortly after his death a memorial was called for. Initially, Amsterdam was the city that was to receive the memorial, but when the town council failed to cooperate, Rotterdam was chosen instead.So in 1915, the Van 't Hoff-monument was unveiled in front of his old school at the 's-Gravendijkwal: a bronze statue placed on a high pedestal, surrounded by two female figures representing Imagination and Reason. The unveiling-ceremony of the fifteen meters wide and nine meters high monument was a very sober affair. Because of the war it was impossible for scholars from outside the country to come to Rotterdam.

## First Traffic Breakthrough

At the beginning of the twentieth century, traffic increased in Rotterdam to such an extent that a major breakthrough was needed in the city. The electric street car required major adaptations within the old Rotterdam with its many alleys and narrow streets. Also the bridges between the river banks were insufficiently processing the streams of people. More often than not the Koninginnebrug was open because the larger ships could no longer pass under the low bridge over the Maas, and it was therefore nicknamed the Brug der Zuchten (Bridge of Sighs). Only increasing the capacity of the bridge would not be enough since this would result in traffic jams in the city center. A fundamental change took place under Mayor A.R. Zimmerman (1869-1939), who turned the Coolsingel into an urban boulevard. The city hall, the main post office and the exchange building would later be built here. In order to carry out these plans the Coolvest had to be filled up and the Zandstraat neighborhood broken down.

The Coolsingel and the Goudsesingel, which ran from north to south, could only function well if the traffic situation in other parts of the city would improve, prompting the need for a new road from east to west. The First World War and lack of funding prevented the plans from being executed.

KEY MOMENT

## A healthy mind in a healthy body

On July 19, 1908, football club Feyenoord was set up, twenty years after Sparta (1888) and six years after Excelsior (1902). Of the three clubs Feyenoord is undoubtedly the most successful.

# Chapter 6

# Between the Two Wars (1914-1940); From Work City to Cultural City

***In This Chapter:***

- The Belgians are coming
- Spy City Rotterdam
- Promenade and town hall
- Living in a garden suburb
- A second large expansion phase
- Painting the town red
- Het Nieuwe Bouwen
- Going under water

Although the Netherlands remain politically neutral during the First World War, the country is definitely confronted with its consequences. Rotterdam enters a turbulent period in time. The city turns out to be very vulnerable in terms of trade as a result of the dependence on the German hinterland and the Rhine. Belgian refugees leave their marks in the city. After the war, Rotterdam becomes a city with a busy nightlife, with the new town hall and the post office at the Coolsingel as the center of town, for which both the area of the Meent and the Coolsingel itself needed a major overhaul. Modern dance halls appear in the city, as well as theaters and cafes. Jazz introduces itself to Rotterdam while at some distance garden villages emerge. Sensational buildings, constructed under the influence of the so-called Nieuwe Bouwen (which literally translated means New Building, a movement or architectural style related to cubism and De Stijl), give the city a whole new look. Artists find inspiration in the bustling city and link up with new trends. The crisis, the arrival of Jewish refugees, the establishment of the Stichting Luchtafweer Rotterdam (Anti-aircraft Foundation Rotterdam) and the claiming of the airfield Waalhaven in the thirties are the harbingers of a new war.

## Rotterdam and the 'Great' War

Particularly in Rotterdam the 'Great' War was noticeable since the city had to deal with trade restrictions and on top of that with a massive influx of refugees. During the first days after the fall of Antwerp on October 7, 1914, some 23,000 Belgians fled to Rotterdam. About 6,000 of them were accommodated by the HAL, the Uranium Company and in public buildings. The rest received shelter in the homes of private people in Rotterdam. After the Belgian capitulation in late November, some 18,000 refugees returned home. Over 5,000 remained in Rotterdam and near the end of the war their number grew to about 9,000. The money needed for their care and housing was provided by the citizens of Rotterdam, but as food was scarce during these bad economic times, this caused a problem with the unemployed of the city, resulting in the looting of potato barges, meat transports and bread carts.

### City of spies

The neutral Netherlands were strategically located between Germany and England. As a port city with many nationalities Rotterdam became a network of international espionage. It was a perfect base for German espionage in Britain and British espionage in Germany and especially in occupied Belgium. The British secret service was housed in the office of the Uranium Company at the Boompjes, the German secret service was stationed in the Imperial German consulate in the White House. The Dutch and particularly some individuals from Rotterdam got involved in espionage and sometimes paid the highest price. On July 30, 1915, Heicke Janssen and Willem Roos, two sailors/spies from Rotterdam, were shot in the Tower of London. However, they did not die for their homeland; they were spying for the Germans. The town was so full of secret agents, spies and smugglers that part of the street between Beurs and Beursstation became known as Spy Corner.

# A New Town Hall

Rarely in the Netherlands and in Rotterdam has any design and layout of a building brought as much commotion as the construction of the new town hall at the Coolsingel. It started with its location. In 1908, Mayor Zimmerman introduced plans to build a new town hall, for which he did not choose the old center at the Cheese Market and Hoogstraat, but rather the Coolsingel, which was more towards the outskirts of the city. The Coolsingel was to be a promenade with the town hall as an expression of the world's largest port city. To realize this plan the Zandstraat neighborhood had to be demolished. In 1913, in response to the competition that was organized, the scale models of various architects were presented, but by a bit of maneuvering the mayor was able to have the work of his friend chosen, the architect Henri Evers. This action provoked a storm of protest that was not only about the undemocratic decision process but also the building itself. It was found to be outdated and unfitting for a modern commercial city.

Yet, in 1914, the first pile went into the ground. Because of various circumstances, such as the outbreak of the First World War, the town hall was only completed six years later, on August 10, 1920.

**Figure 6.1:** View of the dismantling of the area between the Zandstraat and the Coolvest in 1912, the future location of the town hall; photo of B.H.W. Berssen-brugge

The way Rotterdam wanted to present itself as a city cannot only be deduced from the shape of the building but also from the decoration and furnishings. Trade, shipping and administration are represented by many allegorical figures in different places on the exterior. On the front is the Maiden of Rotterdam, surrounded by the arms of the annexed municipalities, and on the tower stands the golden Angel of Peace, a reference to the First World War. The citizens of Rotterdam and many institutions paid for the interior furnishing of the town hall, such as lamps, stained-glass windows, sculptures, wainscoting, pillows, paintings, carpets, clocks and so on. Many artists worked on the decoration. The stained-glass windows in the main hall depict material and spiritual prosperity. Along the sides of the staircase are life-size statues of the counts of Holland Floris V and Willem III, founders of the city of Rotterdam.

## Revolution

After the war, an international economic crisis prevented a speedy recovery. The political developments in Germany and the Russian Revolution had repercussions on the Netherlands and the workers in Rotterdam. Mayor Zimmerman was concerned that the revolution might spread, and he was willing to make concessions to the socialists who he had asked for their cooperation. Pieter Jelles Troelstra, leader of the SDAP, felt strengthened by this fact. On November 11, 1918, during a speech in the Verkooplokaal at the Goudsesingel, he urged the workers to start a revolution. In response to the threatening transfer of power, the national authorities sent soldiers to guard the town hall and other important public buildings. Troelstra had underestimated the power of the religious (Christian) parties and the revolution blew over. Troelstra admitted that he had made an error of judgment. To reduce revolutionary sympathies some social laws were introduced and the dock workers were given an eight-hour working day as well as the Saturday afternoon off and a partial abolition of work at night.

## Garden Suburbs Vreewijk and Heijplaat

During the early twentieth century the idea for garden suburbs for the underprivileged class emerged: quality housing with a village character in the middle of a city quarter, mostly near factories. Both economic and social motives were the basis for this idea. Healthy workers would be sick less often and worked harder. The lack of nightlife and the emphasis on family life would contribute to a better attitude toward work and a healthy lifestyle. For the realization of garden village Vreewijk the NV Eerste Rotterdamse Tuindorp (First Rotterdam Garden Village) was founded by notables in Rotterdam in 1913. The street plan of Vreewijk is based on the original pattern of ditches and trenches of the former polder. The Vliet formed the basis for the canal along the Langegeer. The plan was developed by the renowned architects H.P. Berlage and M.J. Granpré Molière. The first houses were delivered around 1919, but the entire village wasn't finished until the beginning of the Second World War.

Another well-known garden village – and dating to the same period – is Heijplaat, which the Rotterdamsche Droogdok Maatschappij (RDM, Rotterdam Dry-dock Company) realized for her workers after a design of H.A.J. Baanders. Because the employees came from different regions, as many as three churches and two schools were built for the different religious convictions. Furthermore, there were all kinds of amenities when the village was completed in 1920, such as an entertainment center with shops, a house for young bachelors and a bathhouse and laundry facilities. The architecture was diverse, with a distinction between the upper and lower staff where the type of housing was concerned. In 1930, the village was expanded with a quarantine room.

DID YOU KNOW?

## Museum House Vreewijk

Vreewijk has a museum house at the Lede 40. The last resident, who was born there and never moved, left the property in its original state. A shower, central heating and hot water facilities are therefore absent, and the kitchen is still in its original state. The colors and wallpaper have been restored in the old style. The house thus paints a special image of Tuindorp Vreewijk at the beginning of the twentieth century. It also serves as a meeting point for local residents, who can contribute to the collection/interior of the museum with photos, objects and stories. In this way the house can actually become the memory of the neighborhood.

# Urban Breakthrough

After the first traffic breakthrough – from north to south – had been completed at the turn of the century, the second breakthrough followed during the twenties, now from east to west.

## Meent

This breakthrough was realized in two phases. The first phase was the demolition of the narrow streets and buildings at the Meent between the Binnenrotte and the Lombardstraat, including the Paradijskerk (Paradise Church) dating to 1718. The new road was completed in 1929, the same year in which the Meentbrug across the Delftsevaart was completed. The second part of the breakthrough involved the main road Jonker Fransstraat/Coolsingel. In order to realize this part of the operation, the original part of the Meent between the filled-up Gedempte Botersloot and the Oppert needed to be widened and several buildings demolished, resulting in a completely different view of the city. The back of the synagogue, until then wedged between the buildings of the Wildezeesteeg, Tweede Lombardstraat and the Meent, was freed of the adjacent buildings. The economic crisis in the thirties prevented part of the plans from being realized. The new road was never constructed. The whole area remained vacant until 1937, and only then development got underway. When the city was bombed on May 14, 1940, the Meent had still not been completely finished.

## Intersection Hofplein

In those years, the square called Hofplein was an unusually busy intersection with cars, trams, carriages, horses, cyclists and pedestrians. The immediate surrounding area consisted of a crossing of water and land routes from and to the city. The Hofplein-station and rail road traffic also contributed to the chaos. In addition, the Hofplein – with its café Loos and dancing Pschorr with its spectacular glass dance floor at the Coolsingel – was also a renowned center of entertainment and nightlife. Urban planners and architects tried to transform this lively square into a full-blown traffic junction. Architect Berlage made an attempt in 1921, but eventually the plan of city architect W.G. Witteveen (1891-1979) got the green light. The actual work started in 1939, but the outbreak of the war put an end to the realization of the plan.

IMPORTANT

## Delft Gate

In the twentieth century, only the Oostpoort (East Gate) and the Delftse Poort reminded of the old fortifications. The Oostpoort was demolished in 1912. The Delftse Poort, which had been built round 1770 by architect Pieter de Swart, was the last gate standing. Gradually it became an obstacle for the increasingly congested roads around the Hofplein. The town council decided in 1937 not to demolish the last gate but move it instead. Rolling it – in its entirety – was too expensive, so during a period of three months it was taken down brick by brick and then re-built, again brick by brick. Badly damaged by the bombing in May 1940, the remains were pulled down and thrown into the river Rotte. In 1995, near the original site in the heart of Rotterdam, the outlines of the gate were revealed as a steel construction by the artist Cor Kraat.

**Figure 6.2:** The Delftse Poort around 1900; drawing by Anton Dirckx

## Travelling by Spido

Spido is a household name in Rotterdam, although no one really knows what the word means. The Spido harbor service was established late in 1918 by Fop Smit of the Nederlandsche Stoomsleepdienst (Dutch Steam Towing Service) and D.G. van Beuningen, director of the Steenkolen Handels Vereeniging (SHV, Coal Trading Association). Their purpose was to create a regular taxi service for bringing sailors from their home to their ship. Spido also transported workers to and from their work in the harbor at the beginning and at the end of the day. Spido used old ships of the Roeiers Vereeniging Eendracht (Rowing Association Unity) and gave them a new name. Gradually, Spido also took care of mail transport for sailors in other ports. When the Waalhaven airfield – from which sightseeing flights over Rotterdam were organized – was opened to the public in 1922, Spido became part of a day out: the visitors were transported over water to the far-off Waalhaven. Only after the war Spido built a modern fleet.

# Culture in the City

## Culture Park Het Land van Hoboken

The land of Hoboken, measuring 56 hectares and belonging to the shipping family Van Hoboken, was sold to the municipality in 1924. The family had lived on the estate – in the villa Dijkzigt – since 1852. City architect Witteveen designed an urban development plan for this area which he also named Dijkzigt and in which Nature played a major role. Witteveen wanted to use this open space as the counterpart of the harbor and turn it into a cultural park. Modern white villas arose in the park, in the style of the movement called Nieuwe Bouwen, such as the current Chabot Museum. Villa Dijkzigt became the home of the Natural History Museum in 1927 while in 1935 Museum Boijmans moved from the Schielandshuis to the new park. Also the Erasmiaans Gymnasium (Gymnasium Erasmianum) settled in the park.

### Abram Tuschinski

Because of the magnificent Tuschinski Theater, Tuschinski is associated with Amsterdam. Only few people know that Tuschinski started his career in Rotterdam. The difficult situation for the Jews and the prospect of a Russian conscription made Abram Içek Tuschinski (1886-1942) leave his native country Poland. He had arranged to work in Rotterdam as an accomplished tailor and he arrived in the city in 1904. Soon afterwards he sent for his wife Mariem Ehrlich. Tuschinski was famous for his expert work. To help their displaced compatriots, the couple started a pension for emigrants in the Nadorststraat. The pension was called Polska.

Movies, however, were Tuschinski's greatest passion. The movie theaters in the city, he considered shabby. A beautiful theater would attract a larger audience. Tuschinski hired the old sailor church at the Coolvest

– owned by the municipality – refurbished it and provided it with luxury seats. His doormen wore a special outfit. On August 24, 1911, Thalia opened its doors, Tuschinski's first movie theater in the Netherlands. In subsequent years he opened another four cinemas in town. Only after that he dared to take a chance in Amsterdam where he built the Tuschinski Theater in 1921. The crown on his work in Rotterdam was the beautifully decorated Grand Théâtre, the counterpart of the Tuschinski Theater in Amsterdam. It also hosted the chic cabaret-dansant La Gaité and from 1932 the avant-garde movie theater Studio '32. During the bombing of May 14, 1940 (so actually on his birthday), Tuschinski saw how everything was destroyed. In 1942, Tuschinski and his wife were deported to Poland, where they were murdered in Auschwitz.

## Artists in the City

During the twenties and thirties, the modern city of Rotterdam attracted many sophisticated modern artists. They had close links with the industry, but they also introduced their ideas at the Academie van Beeldende Kunsten (Academy of Fine Arts). Under the guidance of head teacher Jacob (Jac.) Jongert, the future artists Piet Zwart, Gerrit Kiljan, Jan Kamman, Dick Elffers and Paul Schuitema worked there. They sympathized with modern art directions, such as the German Bauhaus, De Stijl and Russian Constructivism. Their fundamental idea was to design in a functional and businesslike style. Under the influence of socialist ideas they devoted themselves to machine-made mass products, beautifully shaped and affordable for everyone. These artists were among the founders of the Nieuwe Typografie (New Typography) and Nieuwe Fotografie (New Photography). They experimented with new photo and letter techniques which they applied to the design of advertisements. Thus, Jongert became the designer of the corporate identity for the Van Nelle Factory and Schuitema of Van Berkel's scales and cutting machines.

Rotterdam had some progressive artists' associations. Filmliga released avant-garde films, the architects were united in Opbouw (meaning construction) and the Rotterdam workers and writers collective association Links Richten (Aim Left) and the Vereeniging van Arbeiders Fotografen (VAF, Association of Working Class Photographers) used writings and photography in the political struggle of the proletariat against capitalism. In 1932, the VAF organized the first photo exhibition by Dutch workers in Ons Huis (Our House), a socialist community center.

## Modern Rotterdam and Revolutionary Architecture

The architects of the international movement of the Nieuwe Zakelijkheid (translated as New Objectivity or New Pragmatism, related to the German movement Neue Sachlichkeit) were given a chance in Rotterdam in the field of (public) housing. Their ideological starting point was the functionalist city with four components: living, working, recreation and traffic. Light, air and space were a prerequisite and could be established by using modern materials such as concrete and steel. In order to keep the costs low, prefabricated building elements were used. An example is the Justus van Effenblok (1921) in Spangen, designed by the architect Michiel Brinkman (1873-1925) from Rotterdam. Revolutionary is the gallery – the first in the Netherlands – a raised walkway on the inside of the block along the apartments on the first floor. The Jan Luykenblok and the Witte Dorp (White Village), which takes its name from the white working-class houses, were designed by architect J.J.P. Oud (1890-1963). The White Village was built on a symmetrical triangular street lay-out. The design of the project, the efficient layout and the particular use of color (yellow and blue) won the White Village international fame. Around 1930, in the part of town called Zuid (South), the world famous Kiefhoekcomplex by architect Oud was finished, also designed for the working class. Rotterdam also hosts the first gallery apartments, the Bergpolderflat, built in the mid-thirties by Van Tijen (1894-1974), J.A. Brinkman (1902-1949) and L.C. van der Vlugt (1894-1936), and destined for lower class rental housing. The architectural movement Nieuwe Bouwen includes the Van Nelle Factory (1929) in the Spaanse Polder and the Feyenoord Stadium (1937) in the area called Zuid, by the architects Brinkman and Van der Vlugt; café De Unie (1925) by Oud at the Coolsingel; and De Bijenkorf (1930) by W.M. Dudok (1884-1974) at the Schiedamsevest, at that time the largest department store in the Netherlands.

## The SS Nieuw Amsterdam

The Nieuw Amsterdam was the largest pre-war passenger ship the HAL owned, and it had a stunningly beautiful interior. On April 10, 1937, the ship was launched by Queen Wilhelmina. The contract for designing the interior decoration was awarded to the architects Brinkman and Van der Vlugt. As Van der Vlugt died and Brinkman became seriously ill, the project ran into trouble. The solution came from Willem Hugo de Monchy (1894-1968), director of HAL, who took over the artistic leadership. He came up with a revolutionary plan. Instead of having the entire project handled by one agency, he hired seven interior designers to take care of the interiors. Then each architect chose his own group of artists to deal with the fine-tuning of the interior furnishing. De Monchy was the head of this collective – consisting of some seventy artists whom he was able to inspire to an intensive collaboration. Many of these artists had built up national and sometimes international fame. About one-sixth of them came from Rotterdam, among whom Marius and Han Richters, Jaap Gidding, Willem Gispen, Sybold van Ravesteyn, Hendrik Chabot, Pieter den Besten, Herman Bieling, Leendert Bolle and Lode Sengers, indicating that the Rotterdam art scene at that time could be called sophisticated and progressive.

IMPORTANT

## Boxing and swimming

The Dutch Windmill Bep van Klaveren was a sensation at the 1928 Olympic Games, winning a gold medal, but at the Olympics in Berlin in 1936, the swimmer Rie Mastenbroek from Rotterdam won as many as three gold medals and one silver medal.

# *Nenijto*

In 1928, the Nederlandsche Nijverheidstentoonstelling (Nenijto, Dutch Industry Exhibition) was held as a counterpart of the Olympic Games in Amsterdam. On the grounds behind Station Delftse Poort, four large halls were constructed, designed by C.B. van der Tak. Although the halls were intended for temporary use, after the exhibition they were handed over to the municipality by shipping magnate D.G. van Beuningen. The Metal Hal was moved in 1929 to the Marconiplein as part of the Ford car factory. Until the late forties, Nenijto Hall B remained a focal point for trade fairs, sporting events and other activities, such as the first six-day cycling contest which was held in the specially adapted and heated Nenijto hall in 1936.

DID YOU KNOW?

## Henry Ford in Rotterdam

On October 4, 1930, Henry Ford visited the Ford Factory under construction at the Marconiplein. For one short period it seemed as if Rotterdam was going to be a real car-manufacturing city.
Since the new complex was already advanced to a meter high iron skeleton, a groundbreaking ceremony could no longer be considered appropriate; Henry Ford would lay a memorial stone instead. Upon arrival, Ford was terribly disappointed. He was of the opinion that the factory was far too

small and he refused to lay the stone. So the Ford Motor Company of Holland started negotiations with the municipality for the necessary land to build larger factories on the left bank of the river Maas, which they wanted to exchange for the complex at the Marconiplein. The municipality would then be able to use it as a tram and bus depot. The exchange did not take place and thus the likelihood of a Ford factory was gone. In 1931, Ford decided to establish its company in Amsterdam.

# A New Zoo

In 1855, two railway-employees had set up a little park for pheasants and waterfowl at the Kruiskade. The garden would be the basis for the Rotterdamsche Diergaarde (Zoo) which opened on May 18, 1857. The first director was Henri Martin, an animal trainer famous in all of Europe. Even before the Second World War, it was decided that the zoo, which was now in the middle of the city, would move to Blijdorp. Architect Sybold van Ravesteyn designed a new zoo with ditches and canals instead of fences and bars, and spacious living meadows and heated indoor spaces. In 1938, the old zoo was dismantled, although a small portion remained in use. Just before the devastating bombing of May 14, 1940, the zoo was hit on May 12 by bombs that were meant for Station Delftse Poort. Because almost all the animals had already been transferred to Blijdorp it is a myth that wild animals roamed the streets of Rotterdam after the bombing.

# Maas Tunnel

The Maas Tunnel, which connects the left and the right bank of the river Maas, is the second fixed embankment connection in Rotterdam and the oldest immersed traffic tunnel in the Netherlands. The narrow Willemsbrug and Koninginnebrug (brug means bridge) could not possibly handle the heavy traffic in an orderly way. Since installing a new bridge yielded many technical and financial problems, the municipality opted for a tunnel. Typical are the striking ventilation buildings that stand 35 meters high. Along with the entrance buildings these are the only areas above ground that betray the presence of the Maas Tunnel. The tunnel has two tube systems for motorized traffic. The tubes for bicycles are accessed by stairs with a length of 17 meters. In 1937, the construction works commenced, for which the Norwegian church had to be moved. Despite the bombardment of May 14, 1940, the work continued. On February 14, 1942, after an unofficial secret opening ceremony, the Maas Tunnel was declared open to all traffic.

## Jews in Rotterdam

The persecution of Jews in Germany and Austria brought a stream of refugees to Western Europe, mainly after the Kristallnacht in November 1938. Under pressure from public opinion, they were allowed in the Netherlands, albeit to a limited extent. There were various types of refugee camps in Rotterdam. In Hoek van Holland, the export butcher's shop was used as a shelter and at Heijplaat the quarantine station served as such. A few hundred German Jews stayed in Hoek van Holland, supervised by the Rotterdam police. Usually they were given a temporary residence status, after having been subjected to an investigation. In May 1940, the camp still had 85 residents. The internees at Heijplaat included Claus Plasterk, the father of Minister Ronald Plasterk, and Hannelore Grünberg-Klein, the mother of the writer Arnon Grunberg.

# Chapter 7

# Second World War (1940-1945)

### *In This Chapter:*

- Preparing the bombing
- City on fire
- Debris in canals and inner harbors
- Start of the reconstruction
- Living and shopping in devastated Rotterdam
- Jews deported
- Port facilities demolished
- Operation Rosenstock

Soon after the German invasion of the Netherlands on May 10, 1940, the heavy bombing of Rotterdam follows. A large part of the inner city is destroyed and nearly a thousand people lose their lives. The Allied mistake of bombing Rotterdam West in 1943 and the German destruction of the port facilities in 1944 cause even greater human and material losses. In response to the 'great' bombardment of 1940 a reconstruction plan is prepared, building on the pre-war urban renewal projects. In those first years of the war, especially the Jews become the victims. Almost the entire Jewish community of Rotterdam, with 11,006 Jews one of the largest communities in the Netherlands, is deported and murdered in concentration camps.

Another all-time low in the history of Rotterdam is the raid during the night of November 10, 1944, in which 50,000 men from Rotterdam and Schiedam are deported and put to work in Germany as forced laborers. The ensuing famine (called Hongerwinter in Dutch) in the west costs the lives of thousands more. The German terror continues to rule and actions of resistance and liquidations lead to severe reprisals. On May 5, 1945, the Germans capitulate but in Rotterdam they don't surrender until May 8, when the Allies invade the city. Only then Rotterdam is truly liberated.

## The Attack on Rotterdam Begins

The Germans attacked the Netherlands in the early morning of May 10, 1940. They rapidly seized the military airfield Waalhaven and destroyed most of the buildings. Still, several Fokker aircraft managed to shoot down a few German planes from the Waalhaven airfield. Subsequently twelve German hydroplanes landed on both sides of the bridges over the river Maas, which were crucial – along with the bridges at Moerdijk and Dordrecht – because through that corridor the Germans were able to invade Holland and advance towards Belgium and France. Marines and soldiers were ordered to prevent the passage of German troops. Unfortunately they were unable to recapture the bridges, but they did manage to last a long time, thus preventing the enemy from moving forward. For the Germans, who had intended a rapid advance towards the south, the war around Rotterdam was unexpectedly slow.

## The Ultimatum

On May 14, 1940, General Rudolf Schmidt sent an ultimatum to Colonel P.W. Scharroo, the Dutch commander of Rotterdam, and to P.J. Oud, mayor of Rotterdam. Colonel Scharroo received the letter at 10:30 a.m. The ultimatum was signed 'the commander of the German troops', but without a personal signature or mention of rank. Moreover, the document was full of grammatical mistakes. The ultimatum stated that two hours after receiving the letter, measures would be taken to destroy Rotterdam. Scharroo did not take the unsigned paper seriously. General Winkelman, the commander-in-chief of the Dutch armed forces, told Scharroo to demand a new and better formulated ultimatum, one that had to be signed and bear the name and rank of the German officer. The request reached Oberstleutnant Von Choltitz fifteen minutes before the expiry of the ultimatum. General Schmidt ordered the planned bombing of 13.00 p.m. to be postponed because of surrender negotiations. However, at that very moment the squadron was leaving the German airfields. Opinions vary about what happened from that moment on. One explanation is that it was agreed that if the bombardment would be cancelled, red flares would be fired from the Noordereiland (Northern Island). Schmidt never received notice that the German planes had actually taken off and therefore he took no steps to have the red flares discharged. He had the ultimatum drafted again, signed with name, rank, and signature and added that the surrender by Scharroo needed to be received by 16.20 p.m. At that moment it was 13.20 p.m.

## Rotterdam under Fire

The Germans feared the persistent opposition from the Dutch side and therefore decided to execute a large surface bombardment. It was regarded as a means of speeding up the Dutch surrender. The 54 Heinkels set course for Rotterdam according to plan and, because they saw no red flares, dropped their bombs over the city. On May 14, at 13:27 p.m., the center of town, Kralingen, the Proveniers-district, the area called Oude Noorden (Old North) and the Lis-quarter, were destroyed in barely fifteen minutes by 97,000 kilos of Brisant bombs. In consultation with Mayor Oud, colonel Scharroo decided that Rotterdam would capitulate. To prevent other cities from being bombed, the Netherlands fully surrendered on May 15, 1940.

The bombing of the city caused a huge fire, which was able to spread fast because of the strong wind. A total of 800 to 900 people perished, about 30,000 homes and businesses were destroyed and nearly 80,000 inhabitants of Rotterdam lost their homes. During those early days of May, the Dutch armed forces lost a total of 185 soldiers in Rotterdam and the surrounding area. It took until May 16 for the major fires to be extinguished. In an area of over 250 hectares virtually everything had been destroyed.

## Clearing the Debris

The Municipal Technical Department (GTD) was told by the mayor and the town council – by order of the Germans – to clear the debris from the city. Initially this was done by some 30,000 unemployed people, but from the end of May the new removal division of the GTD did the job, working in shifts in six districts. Also the Building Police, demolition companies and the army were brought in to clear the area as quickly as possible. On November 1, 1940, the cleaning operation was nearly completed and the dismantling of the foundations could begin. About 3 million cubic meters of rubble was transported to landfill sites and would later be used to fill the Rotterdam Schie, the Schiedamsesingel, Blaak and Kolk. During these filling-operations the director of Public Works, Witteveen, kept in mind his pre-war plans for urban expansion. Only a few buildings in the city emerged from the bombing without too much damage: the White House, the Schielandshuis, Town Hall and the post office, the HBU-building, Hotel Atlanta, the town library, the outside of the Laurenskerk, part of the Bijenkorf department store and the theater. The theater and the Bijenkorf were later demolished nonetheless.

**Figure 7.1:** (1940) View of the immediate surroundings of the Sint Laurenskerk, struck by German bombs; the Steigersgracht is in the foreground

# *Plans for Reconstruction*

A few days after the bombing, Witteveen was commissioned by the town council to develop a reconstruction plan. His plan was in fact a continuation of the pre-war plan he had developed. On June 21, 1940, Witteveen explained his plan to the Dutch and German officials. He had taken the historic city triangle as basis, but instead of the original 25,000 houses only 10,000 houses would be rebuilt. Companies would not return to the city center but would find a place somewhere in the polders, which had been expropriated for this purpose. Also the annexation of the bordering communities of IJsselmonde, Overschie, Schiebroek and Hilligersberg and parts of neighboring municipalities – which had already been planned before the war – now became reality. The district on the right bank of the Maas thus became nearly twice as large. As the war progressed, other architects got involved in the project. They and others criticized the reconstruction plan of Witteveen, who eventually withdrew. Cornelis van Traa was then commissioned to develop a new plan.

## Emergency Shops and Housing

As a result of the bombardment, a large part of the shops in the center had been demolished. As for the time being building new stores was out of the question, temporary shops were set up on the edge of downtown. The Municipal Technical Services prepared 223 small emergency stores, which were grouped in rows of five to ten. They could be hired from the municipality. They were simple but fairly solid structures, which were built on the sidewalks. A temporary pub was often part of such a row of shops. The walls of the small buildings were sometimes decorated with paintings by artists. Larger companies were allowed to rent plots of land near Dijkzigt and Blijdorp, where they could construct their new buildings.

Temporary housing appeared outside the center of Rotterdam. The houses were built at the end of 1940 for thousands of citizens who still had not been able to find decent shelter. They carried names such as Utrechts Dorp (dorp means village) and Gelders Dorp, both located along the Noorderkanaal (Northern Canal), and Brabants Dorp near the Zuidplein (South Square) on the left bank of the river. Emergency housing was also set up at the Gordelweg in Smeetsland in the still independent IJsselmonde, in the Babberspolder in Vlaardingen and in Overschie, where the complex Landzicht still exists. The total amounted to more than a thousand homes. These houses were meant to provide temporary shelter, but the housing shortage persisted until after the war and some villages were therefore inhabited longer than originally intended. Brabants Dorp lasted until the sixties, when it was finally demolished to clear the way for the construction of the Ikazia Hospital and the subway, and the dwellings in Smeetsland even survived until 2010.

**Figure 7.2:** Street scene with many horse carriages in the summer of 1940; drawing by Herman Schotel

# Loods 24

The first deportations of Dutch Jews began in July 1942. In Rotterdam, they had to check in at Loods 24, a wooden transit warehouse behind a more than two meters high wall on the enclosed port area of the Gemeentelijke Handelsinrichtingen (Municipal Commercial Establishments) in Zuid, between the Spoorweghaven and the Binnenhaven. Through the transit yard Feijenoord a rail connection joined the national rail network. The first transport, with over 1,000 Jews, left for Westerbork on the night of July 30, 1942. More deportations followed later in 1942 and in 1943. Of the 8368 'full Jews' (having four Jewish grandparents) who lived in Rotterdam, 6790 arrived in Westerbork through Loods 24. In the death camps in Eastern Europe almost everyone was killed. At the place where Loods 24 once stood, the vacant square Plein Loods 24 and the nearby remains of the wall of the Municipal Commercial Establishments remind us of the deportations. In 2013, the Joods Kindermonument (Jewish Children's Memorial) at the Stieltjesstraat was added as a monument.

## The Forgotten Bombardment

During the war, Rotterdam suffered hundreds of Allied air raids. The heaviest bombing after that of May 14, 1940, was the one on the west part of Rotterdam on March 31, 1943. Just after noon of that day, the neighborhood of Bospolder-Middendijken was hit by an American air strike. Within a short time a large number of heavy bombs were dropped in the densely populated area, resulting in the deaths of 400 people while 13,000 lost their homes. The cause of the accidental bombardment was the stiff wind on the ground in combination with heavy clouding. The bombs were meant for ships and installations in the industrial area between the Keilehaven and Merwehaven. The Wilton-Feijenoord shipyard was actually a manufacturing plant of torpedo launching tubes for German U-boats. The bombing was intended to weaken the German war industry. Because in general the term 'the bombing' is used to refer to the bombardment of May 14, 1940, this accidental bombing was named The Forgotten Bombardment.

## The Quays Come Tumbling down

Already during the first days of the war in May 1940, the port of Rotterdam had suffered a lot of damage to sheds and warehouses. The Allied bombings in the years that followed caused even more damage, but the largest destruction by far occurred in late September 1944. The Germans were worried by the rapid Allied advance in Belgium, whereby – on September 4 – the port of Antwerp had fallen into the hands of the Allies undamaged and the first liberation troops had reached the Dutch border. That very same day, Hitler ordered that the ports of Amsterdam and Rotterdam had to be destroyed. The intention was not to completely destroy all of the port facilities, but only to remove the essential elements of the cranes and thus paralyze the port. On the night of September 22, several docks at the municipal yard were sunk and machine installations destroyed. On the 25th of September, bombs were placed on the left bank of the river, and the residents of Katendrecht had to leave their homes. The bombs exploded on September 27. The quays along the Rijnhaven and the north side of the Maashaven were blown up. On September 28, the quay along the Waalhaven was destroyed, including the German submarine base. New explosions followed a day later. This time the residents of the garden village Heijplaat had to evacuate. In the Rijnhaven quay walls collapsed, and sheds and cranes toppled and landed in the water. The Wilhelminakade was largely destroyed, as were the quay walls along the Rijnhaven, the north side of the Maashaven, the Waalhaven and the west side of the Merwehaven; in total approximately 7000 meters of quay was blown to smithereens. The damage to lifting equipment such as cranes and ramps was huge and many sheds and warehouses were lost.

## Sabotage in the Harbor

Several assault teams (squads, gangs) were active in Rotterdam, operating as part of the Landelijke Knokploegen (LKP, national assault teams or squads). By raids on distribution centers and civil registration offices they got hold of ration cards and identity documents. They released resistance fighters from prisons, liquidated traitors, and blew up bridges and railways in order to hinder the German occupiers whenever possible. Of great importance was the harbor sabotage. The Germans tried to block the port of Rotterdam and the Nieuwe Waterweg by sinking ships. To avoid a blockage, the assault teams tried – as much as possible – to blow up the designated vessels. The harbor was thus never completely paralyzed and the occupying forces never managed to block the Nieuwe Waterweg. Of the 200-meter wide Nieuwe Waterweg, a narrow navigable channel remained open, measuring about 45 meters wide and approximately 7.5 meters deep. It was not much, but the attempt to close the Nieuwe Waterweg must certainly be considered a failure.

## A narrow escape

The demolition of the harbor was known to the government, but not to its full extent. Through the Resistance, the request came to give further information about the destruction. Nico Koomans, director of the Port Authority, was willing to do so. He was taken to the liberated city of Eindhoven and told his story to representatives of the Allies, after which he returned to Rotterdam. The Germans, however, were aware of the case but Koomans managed to escape arrest because the Sicherheitsdienst (SD) could not find his house. The family Koomans lived at the Prinses Julianalaan, but during the war the occupying forces had changed all the street names that reminded of the royal family. Thus, the Prinses Julianalaan had become the Vredehoflaan. However, the arrest warrant was issued for the Julianalaan. The confusion gave Koomans, after having been tipped off, enough time to go into hiding.

## Bombardments

During the Second World War, Rotterdam suffered at least 250 bombardments, mostly from the German side, but there were also bombings by the Allies. Throughout the war, Rotterdam has had to deal with 102 Allied air raids, killing more than 830 civilians.

# Raids

The Nazi regime tried to fill the vacant jobs in Germany with manpower from the occupied territories, the process was called Arbeitseinsatz. The landings in Normandy intensified the Arbeitseinsatz. On November 10 and 11, 1944, raids took place in Rotterdam and Schiedam of which the size and result would be unique in the Netherlands. In the early morning of Friday, November 10, the Germans began their operation Rosenstock by sealing off Schiedam and the Rotterdam districts Schiebroek, Hillegersberg, Kralingen, Spangenberg as well as the city center. The Germans combed the area block by block, neighborhood by neighborhood and street by street, looking for men between 17 and 40 years old. On November 10, they searched Schiedam, Rotterdam Zuid and the northern suburbs. The next day the center of town was subjected to a similar raid. Some 8,000 German soldiers were deployed in this surprise action. Intimidated by the Germans, many people surrendered out of fear. More than 50,000 citizens of Rotterdam and Schiedam were thus deported.

# Free at Last

From the 5th of May, the official Liberation Day, the Dutch Interior Forces were operating in the city. In several places they got into fights with German troops. The Germans only wanted to officially surrender to the Allies. Rotterdam became the stage for a shootout between the armed resistance forces and the Kriegsmarine, German marines. On May 7, the German commander had still not capitulated, but the commanders of the Interior Forces had already moved into the town hall. Mayor Oud, who was fired in 1941, was brought from his home at the Hoflaan to the town hall. By then the NSB-mayor Müller had already been arrested. Thousands of people at the Coolsingel witnessed the return of the mayor. Even Prince Bernhard paid a quick visit to the city. On May 8, the Allies finally entered Rotterdam. That very moment signaled the German capitulation in Rotterdam and the retreat of the German troops.

## Crooswijk General Cemetery, Kerkhoflaan 5

During the Second World War, thousands of citizens from Rotterdam as well as soldiers found their final resting place at the Crooswijk General Cemetery. Several monuments remind us of them. Two fields of honor with graves of Dutch soldiers and one for the Allied forces have been given a place in the cemetery. Another large field of honor, containing 115 graves, commemorates soldiers who were killed during the fighting in 1940 and yet another field holds the graves of the 12 soldiers who died during the bombing of Rotterdam. A long line of headstones displays the names of the soldiers and the date on which they died. The memorial Cross of Sacrifice commemorates the fallen military forces on the Allied side: 124 British soldiers and five from Poland. The monument 'Vallende man' (Falling Man), made by Cor van Kralingen and unveiled on May 26, 1951, commemorates the Dutch soldiers who died during the occupation of Rotterdam in May 1940 and the later years of the war. 'Knielende vrouw met duif' (Kneeling woman with dove), also by Cor van Kralingen, honors the civilian casualties from the early days in May, 1940. The monument was unveiled exactly 25 years after the bombing, on May 14, 1965. In the back of the base is a bronze box containing a list of 677 names of the bombing victims. In 1943, this cemetery also received the remains of those who died during the Forgotten Bombardment on March 31 and later the victims of the famine. The cemetery also contains several monuments for resistance fighters and civilians who were executed by the Germans.

# Chapter 8
# Reconstruction (1945-1975)

***In This Chapter:***

- The port as spearhead
- Rotterdam builds
- Tourists in the city
- May 18, Construction Day
- The city overflows
- Window on the Maas
- Reconstruction manifestations
- A new concert hall

After the liberation, Rotterdam can start working on its reconstruction. The harbors have top priority. From the fifties, the seaport industry expands further and further to the west, thereby increasing the distance to the city. The shortage of houses is being solved by building new, modern housing estates on the outskirts of the city. To connect these neighborhoods, new roads need to be constructed urgently. During the seventies, the so-called diamond interchange around Rotterdam is created; a set of four- and six-lane intersection-free motorways, including the Van Brienenoordbrug and the Benelux Tunnel. The south of Rotterdam on the left bank is becoming increasingly important, but the tunnel and bridge connections between the north and south parts of the city with their new residential and commercial areas cause many problems. The solution is a modern means of transport: a largely underground subway. Because of the post-war efforts, cleaning-up the old nineteenth-century neighborhoods had moved to the bottom of the priority list. In response – around 1970 – community organizations arise advocating for urban renewal. The environment and environmental pollution are also given due consideration. Meanwhile, the first migrant workers have arrived: first the Spanish workers, followed by Turkish and Moroccan guest workers and Cape Verdean sailors. In the early seventies, the pop festival in Kralingen, the European Cup and the World Cup won by Feyenoord, and Poetry International usher in different times.

## Reconstruction and Expansion of the Ports

Even after the war, economic relations with Germany remained very important. The major petrochemical industry required transshipment capacity. The plans for the first port and industrial area, the Botlek area, date back to 1947. Since Botlek is located west of the river Maas, port activities directed themselves more towards the coast. During Vice Mayor Gerard Ewout van Walsum, who took office in 1952, the development of the Botlek area started with oil supply and distribution.

Between 1958 and 1964, Europoort was built, a new port area suitable for large tankers, located south of the Nieuwe Waterweg on the island Rozenburg. This happened not only at the expense of the village Blankenburg with its 400 inhabitants, but also of the bird sanctuary De Beer and many farms. Europoort, together with the Botlek area, is one of the largest petrochemical industrial areas of the world. In 1962, Rotterdam became the largest port city of the world.

During the sixties, the expertise of container storage and container transfer developed, supplanting the labor-intensive nonbulk cargo transshipment. The reclamation of the so-called Maasvlakte in the Maas estuary began in 1963. The Maasvlakte was designed as a new port area suitable for receiving supertankers. It is located directly at the mouth of river Maas where it meets the North Sea, beyond Europoort. Both the container storage and the Maasvlakte were realized under Mayor Wim Thomassen. In 1966, the first container ship entered the port area. Unlike Botlek and Europoort, the Maasvlakte does not contain oil refineries but has storage tanks instead. Through pipelines, the terminal is connected to the hinterland. The Maasvlakte was completed in the seventies.

DID YOU KNOW?

### Fossils in the plain

The Maasvlakte (vlakte means plain, lowlands) was constructed by building an enclosing embankment, which was then filled with sand from the North Sea. The sand now forms the actual plain and it still contains many fossils. The area is therefore very popular with fossil hunters.

## Tourism during the Reconstruction

'Visit Rotterdam' was the urgent advice of the Rotterdam tourist office in 1947. But how would one tempt a tourist to visit a bombed city during the late forties? It was done by using one magic word: expectation. Although people still grieved for the lost places, they also regarded the new city center as particularly interesting, because it was still full of promise. That city was to be admired best from Het Witte Huis (the White House), where the 'clean slate' was visible all around. One of the first new buildings which the tourists certainly had to visit was the building block called Wereldhaven (World Port) along the Goudsesingel, on which work had started in 1941. Together with the adjacent uniform housing blocks, modern times splashed from the walls. Combined with the wide roads, they announced the new era.

But initially the city center remained empty, except for the pre-war landmarks and some of the new bank buildings. A big attraction for tourists were the so-called 'guided reconstruction tours', which took place during the summer months. They became so popular that they were held twice a day in 1950, attracting some 12,000 visitors in those three months. A year later, the number had risen to over 49,000. Yet, tourism did not increase much. Shopping in the city center wasn't a lot of fun at that time and the lack of entertainment in the evenings also left its mark.

DID YOU KNOW?

### German tourists

Well into the fifties of the past century, the majority of foreign tourists in Rotterdam were from Germany.

## *Stronger through Struggle*

In 1948, the city of Rotterdam was given the motto 'Sterker door Strijd' (Stronger through Struggle) by Queen Wilhelmina as a reminder of the courage and strength that had led the people of Rotterdam through the trials of war and for the significant role that the city had played in the liberation of the country. From that time on, the words 'Stronger through Struggle' shine in the coat of arms on a white ribbon under the city shield. The motto was meant to be accompanied by a sculpture that would be donated by the queen. For this purpose, a competition was held on the theme 'Stronger through Struggle', which was won by the sculptor Hans Hank. The Carrara marble of which the statue was made came from Italy and because of the complicated monetary conditions it was exchanged for a large number of tulip bulbs. The block of marble was so huge it had to be cut in half in order to enter the town hall. The smallest part of the two was intended as a base.

The statue depicts David, not killing Goliath with a stone from his sling, but knocking out the German eagle with a wooden club. The statue was made in the town hall, in the women's restroom in fact. When the statue was taking shape, Hank Hans got into an argument with Mayor Oud, who wanted to give it a place in a corner. But the sculptor had intended the statue for a space where it could be seen from all sides. Eventually she was able to convince the mayor. The unveiling took place on November 30, 1951, by Queen Juliana. The naked David caused a lot of excitement, especially with the religious part of the visitors. After all, in 1949, twelve nudes by Kees van Dongen had been removed from Museum Boijmans.

## Construction Day

From 1947 to 1970, Construction Day was celebrated each year on May 18. During a series of 'construction days' the most diverse objects were presented: from houses to civil works, from road construction to commercial properties, from port development to cultural events and social activities. The Construction Days were meant to evoke an image of a totally new urban life realized by government, industry and citizens together, in harmony: an image of a bright start after a deep darkness, an image showing that people would not just sit and do nothing amidst ruins, rubble and vacant lots. The main intention was to create a new and vibrant city not just for the current residents, but especially for posterity, a city where people would like to live and work. Each of these Construction Days brought new records with it. The initiative had already been born during the war under the name of Stichting Rotterdam 1940. Pioneers of the project were K.P. van der Mandele, president of the Chamber of Commerce and Industry, and Mayor Oud. They had in mind the restoration of the city, particularly in the field of commerce. After the war, collaboration came about between the municipality, commercial enterprises and citizens, resulting in the grand manifestations Ahoy'50, E'55 and the Floriade (1960) as well as the annual Construction Days.

The date of May 18 was chosen because on May 18, 1940, city architect Witteveen had been commissioned for the design of the new city. Rotterdam did not commemorate its destruction – it would do so later on – but celebrated its construction days instead. As the first Construction Day – May 18, 1947 – fell on a Sunday, it was celebrated on May 17. In the presence of Mayor Oud, work began on placing a scaffolding around the ruins of the Sint Laurenstoren (Saint Lawrence Tower); the first piles were driven into the ground for the industrial building along the Goudsesingel and for the Groothandelsgebouw' (Trade Building); the first stone was laid for new homes in Kralingen; new people moved into the five hundredth house in the district called Carnisse and the reconstruction exhibition 'Rotterdam Straks' (straks means later) opened at the Museum Boijmans. Other spectacular moments on Construction Days included the opening of the Leuvesluis (lock or sluice) in 1950 and the Central Station in 1957, and the opening of the relocated ancient inn called 'In den Rustwat' (rest-a-bit) in 1960. The first stone was laid for the new shopping center in Hoogvliet in 1960, construction began on four giant oil storage tankers in Europoort in 1963 and in 1966 the opening of De Doelen took place. Around 1970, the process of reconstruction was considered complete.

## Ahoy'50

The first major public event – Rotterdam Ahoy' in 1950 – takes us to the period of the reconstruction manifestations. Ahoy' is actually an ancient call used by sailors looking out over seas and oceans. Ahoy' became the call of Rotterdam, focusing the attention of the public on the fact that the industrial life of Rotterdam had been restored within a few years after the major bombardments on the city in 1940 and the harbor in 1944. The goal of the public event was to show the entire world how the harbor had been restored, in such a short time and under such difficult circumstances. The most modern port of Europe presented itself under the name Ahoy'50 from June 15 to August 15, 1950. The event was held on the grounds of Dijkzigt and in the Park to emphasize the contact between the harbor and the city. The last of the Nenijto-halls, hall B, was used as an exposition hall and for that purpose it was transported to the grounds of Dijkzigt. The enormous hall, measuring 120 by 60 meters, was actually designated to be dismantled anyway as a result of new plans concerning the area of the Central Station. It was given the name Ahoy Hall. Ahoy'50 united the fields of trade, industry and art. One of the major attractions was a bright-colored sculpture by Karel Appel – 'an explosion of primal forces' – as well as a large scale model of the port. The hall had been decked out with the contributions of various fields of enterprise. The centre piece was the contribution by ship-owners and agents: an indoor pool – measuring 25 by 15 meters – held models of all 324 vessels that had Rotterdam as their home port at that very moment. The number of daily visitors from the Netherlands itself and abroad was so overwhelming that the whole event had to be extended by another two weeks. The manifestation attracted more than one-and-a-half million visitors. A consistent problem during the event was the lack of adequate accommodation for guests. After all, most of the hotels and other guest-houses had been destroyed by the bombardments. The completion of the hotels Atlanta and Regina improved the situation considerably but it was still not enough.

## Crowded City

Gradually the details of the city were filled in. The plan by architect Cornelis van Traa determined the urban layout of modern Rotterdam. In his plans, Van Traa put the focus on areas in the west part of Rotterdam because he felt that his predecessor Witteveen had not reserved enough space for commercial enterprises and retail stores. Van Traa designed a grid of main thoroughfares and connecting roads and roundabouts, and he opened up the Coolsingel as a central promenade towards the river Maas. Before the war, the river had been barely visible from the town. A major project that received international attention because of its special pedestrian zones was the construction of the Lijnbaan (1949-1953). The shopping and residential center was designed by the architects Van den Broek and Bakema. Also in 1953, the Groothandelsgebouw (Trade Building) by architect H.A. Maaskant was completed, as well as the helicopter airfield Heliport enabling flights to Antwerp to take off from Rotterdam. The monument Destroyed City, by Ossip Zadkine, was revealed, the first modern sculpture in the city, and the Historical Museum opened its doors in the Schielandshuis. The new department store De Bijenkorf, a building by Marcel Breuer and Jaap Alsace, was opened in 1957 and a metal sculpture by Naum Gabo was placed in front of it. The Central Station – also opened in 1957 – was one of the last major assignments of Sybold van Ravesteyn.

On May 18, 1966, in the presence of Queen Juliana, concert hall De Doelen was officially opened. The concert hall is seen as an end point in the process of reconstruction, but the city still looked like a Swiss cheese, full of holes. For a very long time the city remained riddled with empty spots. It is now hard to imagine, but in the late eighties an entire deer park was situated where we now find the Weena with the Central Station and the Trade Building.

## The End of the Ahoy Hall

After the successful manifestation Ahoy'50, the actual Ahoy Hall was used for various concerts, anniversaries, exhibitions and trade fairs, such as Femina, but also for providing shelter to the victims of the flood in 1953 and for demonstrations, such as the one against the Russian invasion of Hungary in 1956. The hall was used again during the construction manifestations E'55, the Floriade and C'70. At E'55, the National Energy Manifestation, the Energy Hall was added to the Ahoy Hall. Many companies proudly displayed their new inventions and products, and the visitors could admire the exhibition grounds from a cable car. In 1960, the end of the war by then already fifteen years ago, the Floriade was launched, a horticultural exhibition. The biggest attraction was the Euromast, at that time the tallest building in Rotterdam. From the Ahoy Hall, a cable car ran to the foot of the Euromast. The fourth reconstruction manifestation C'70 (Communication 1970) stretched like a ribbon of two-and-a-half kilometers throughout the city center. C'70 was meant to show that Rotterdam was not only a working-city, but also a city to live in. Meanwhile, the Ahoy Hall was moved in 1966 because of the construction of the Medical Faculty at Dijkzigt. It was given a place at the Heliport terrain, which had been closed in 1965. During C'70 it housed a fair. Part of the hall had already been dismantled by then and served as a roof over the Dolfirodam at the Leuvehaven, a floating dolphin show. The hall was taken apart even further. Since it had already been moved to various locations and had always served as an urban facility, it was decided that the hall would become a permanent establishment in Zuid (South): the Sports and Exhibition Complex Ahoy' opened in 1971.

DID YOU KNOW?

### Restoration of the Saint Lawrence Church

The Sint-Laurenskerk (St. Lawrence Church) had been the spiritual center of the city since the Middle Ages. Its ruins – after the fire of May 14, 1940 – were an accusation against the barbaric violence committed during the war. Because of this 'tradition', the church could not be replaced by new buildings, but had to be rebuilt. In 1952, Queen Juliana laid the foundation stone for the rebuilding of the church. The scaffolding that had been placed around the tower in 1947 was finally removed. It took until 1968 to complete the work on the nave of the church.

## *Living in New Neighborhoods*

Rotterdam's new housing estates outside the center were set up according to the neighborhood concept: small and neatly arranged neighborhoods that were separated from the city and each other by green areas. Three garden suburbs were thus designed for the district called Zuid (South): Pendrecht, Zuidwijk and Lombardijen. Essential part of the plan was the development of the Zuidpark (South Park). The idealistic urban designer Lotte Stam-Beese, working for the Department of Urban Development and Reconstruction, shaped the plans for the expansion project Kleinpolder in Overschie. The new district was intended for workers from the nearby industrial area Spaanse Polder (Spanish Polder). The plan was to provide new, modern houses and buildings based on an open architectural lay-out, community gardens, various neighborhood facilities and the separation of working and living. Stam-Beese used various forms of housing and built living blocks for large and small families, seniors and singles. A new element was a residential area where cars were not allowed to enter. Stam-Beese made similar plans for neighborhoods like Pendrecht, Hoogvliet, Alexanderpolder and Ommoord.

A different residential area was the village of Hoogvliet, which had already been annexed in 1934. In 1947, it received the status of satellite city: an independent residential area instead of just an urban extension. It was supposed to accommodate 60,000 people. Hoogvliet was primarily intended for employees working in the nearby petroleum harbors in the Botlek area.

## De Doelen

In 1952, the plans for building a multi-purpose concert and congress hall were initiated, but only in 1958 the council decided to build what later would become De Doelen (which literally translated means 'the targets', stemming from the late medieval place where the archer guilds used to practice). During the design phase, the architects – in this case the brothers Herman and Evert Kraaijvanger and Rein Fledderus – developed a plan for an underground parking garage. In 1962, the first piles were driven into the ground. The rectangular building had a façade measuring 115 meters and a side wall of nearly 90 meters, and the ideal shape of the actual concert space needed to be found in order to get the best possible acoustics. The opening of De Doelen took place on May 18, 1966, the traditional post-war Construction Day. The indoor car park was inaugurated in the morning, while in the evening – in the presence of Queen Juliana – a gala concert by the Rotterdam Philharmonic Orchestra represented the official opening of the building.

The naming of the building had been a controversial issue. The press and the public came up with many suggestions. The name Rotterdams Concertgebouw (Rotterdam Concert Building/Hall) received a lot of criticism, especially from the concert hall in Amsterdam. In a letter to the mayor and the town hall officials, the Concertgebouw declared that the name of this music temple in Amsterdam and its Concertgebouw Orchestra was a well-known concept all over the world. Nancy Zeelenberg, council member for the arts, also endured some criticism – particularly from the PvdA (Partij van de Arbeid or Labour Party) – when she proposed to name the building De Doelen. They opposed the name because it was historically linked to the better-off, while the municipal music hall was meant to attract a wide audience. The municipality finally decided and – on June 19, 1965 – named the building De Doelen. This kept alive the memory of the old Groote Doelenzaal which once stood at the Coolvest but was destroyed by the bombing in May 1940.

KEY MOMENT

## Smallest subway system

On February 9, 1968, Princess Beatrix and Prince Claus officially inaugurated the first subway network in the Netherlands. It was the smallest subway system in the world. By now it has become a full-fledged public transport network with east-west and north-south lines.

## Erasmus University

The roots of the Erasmus University can be found in the Nederlandse Handels-Hoogeschool (Netherlands School of Commerce), established by private initiative in 1913. In 1939, the name was changed to Nederlandse Economische Hogeschool (Netherlands School of Economics). The road to becoming an academic institution was long and followed two tracks: an economic and a medical track. To meet the need for higher medical education, the Stichting Klinisch Hoger Onderwijs te Rotterdam was established in 1950 (Foundation for Clinical Higher Education), which culminated in 1966 in the Medical Faculty Rotterdam. During the sixties, the faculties of Law and Social Sciences were added to the Netherlands School of Economics, and later the faculties of Philosophy and Business Administration. The road to becoming a university lay ahead, but it took until February 1, 1973, for the Erasmus University to become reality.

IMPORTANT

### 1970: 25 years of liberation

In 1970, Feyenoord was the first Dutch football club to win the European Cup and the World Cup. Kralingen competed with Woodstock during a three day music festival, from June 26 to 29. Despite the pouring rain an estimated 100,000 people came to the Kralingse Bos to listen to pop groups like Jefferson Airplane, Santana, Canned Heat, The Byrds, Pink Floyd and Dr. John. There were also some Dutch performances such as Super Sister, CCC Inc., Focus, Ekseption and Oscar Benton. Slightly earlier, from June 17 to 21, Poetry International took place, the first festival for poetry lovers.

# Chapter 9

# Rotterdam Metropolis (1975-present)

### *In This Chapter:*

- Riots in the Afrikaander neighborhood
- Railway Tunnel
- Developments in Zuid
- The new heart of Rotterdam
- From Beurstraverse to Markthal
- Openbaar Lichaam Rijnmond
- Prostitution
- Opzoomeren
- From Manhattan to RIO on the Maas
- Fire boundary

The long period of reconstruction and economic growth comes to an end in the seventies due to the economic crisis. In the new era, port expansion and industrial growth are no longer guaranteed. A new course is needed. Somewhere in the eighties the focus shifts to qualitative change. Rotterdam is more than just a working city. A major urban renewal follows, making the city a more attractive place and habitat. Downtown shopping areas are developed and new cultural institutions settle in the city. Outside the city center the desolate port areas are being redeveloped. One of these ambitious projects is the so-called Kop van Zuid, where attempts are made to combine living, working and leisure time. To maintain and strengthen the position of world port, an expansion of the port and industrial complex is necessary. Thus, the second Maasvlakte (plain of the river Maas) is realized, an expansion project in the sea. The decision not to reconstruct the city center after the great bombardment causes a break with the historic cityscape. Rotterdam constantly needs to reinvent itself. What is Rotterdam and what does the city want to be? The courage to be a big city with metropolitan flair was already present during the period between the two wars. Has Rotterdam become an international port with a broad view of the world, a metropolis, 'tilting in backlight' as Jules Deelder described the city? Because of the high rise buildings Rotterdam is nicknamed Manhattan on the Maas. Meanwhile, the city's DNA aims for 'Raw, International and Enterprising (rauw, internationaal en ondernemend: rio). Manhattan on the Maas has become RIO on the Maas. And those high-rise buildings? They're multiplying!

## Harbor Town and Multicultural City

As a harbor town where people from all over the world have been pouring in and out for centuries, Rotterdam is primarily a multicultural city. This cohabitation of different cultures generally went well, until in 1972 a small spark ignited a fire. The Afrikaanderwijk (an old working-class neighborhood in the district of Feyenoord) became the scene of clashes between native citizens and Turkish immigrants – hence the name Turkenrellen (Turkish Riots) – which lasted for days. A Dutch woman was put on the street by her Turkish landlord because he wanted to convert the building into a boarding house for immigrant workers. This met with fierce opposition from the dockworkers. A common complaint was that newlywed couples had to wait for years to get a rented house, while slumlords were buying more and more buildings to house foreign workers. The dockworkers of Rotterdam actually spoke up rather frequently. The harbor strike in 1970 was the biggest wildcat-strike (not supported by the trade union movement) after the war. On Friday August 28, more than ten thousand dockworkers laid down their work. The strike lasted three weeks. The strikers had no faith in the union, which did little to improve their working conditions and position. Small left-wing parties, including the SP, set themselves up as action leaders. Their slogans were: 'Their struggle, our struggle' and 'Time for Action' (tijd voor aksie). The door to negotiations was no longer ajar. The Kommunistiese Eenheidsbeweging Nederland (KEN, Communist Unity Movement of the Netherlands), founded in January 1970 by pipefitter Daan Monjé and businessman Nico Schrevel, both from Rotterdam, achieved national fame and a growing number of followers when they decided to support the strike. The harbor strike gave the impulse to numerous national campaigns and reached even beyond the borders. As the majority of the new party members consisted largely of students, an intellectual and a proletarian group arose within the party. The proletarian group led by Daan Monjé split off from the mother party and his group formed the basis of the later Socialist Party (SP). As their weapon in the class struggle, KEN had their magazine Red Tribune, while the SP-magazine was called Tribune.

## Quist's Box

In 1947, the temporary theater designed by architect H. Sutterland was opened at the Aert van Nesstraat. This theater, the Rotterdamsche Schouwburg, was built from the rubble of the bombing, which gave the building a strong symbolic value. It was demolished in 1984 to make way for a new theater at the Schouwburgplein (Theater Square), to which the architect Wim Quist had also added offices, shopping and restaurant facilities, a theater-cafe and 83 homes. The symmetrical building-complex, made up of box-like structures, soon got the name Kist van Quist (kist means box or crate). The lay-out differs from the traditional theaters, as this particular building had a height restriction at the back of the theater due to the homes behind it. Thus the 34-meter high stage tower and the stage floor were installed above the entrance on the side of the square. On April 15, 1988, Elco Brinkman, Minister of Welfare, Health and Culture, opened the new theater. The most recent large building constructed at the Schouwburgplein is the cinema complex Pathé Rotterdam, which opened on March 27, 1996.

**Figure 9.1:** Bridges over the river Maas; drawing by Charles Kemper, 1962

# *Breaking and Building*

Listen, here beats the new heart of Rotterdam. Over the years, this slogan has graced many a construction site. A reflection on the process of reconstruction led to a revision of the course, but not to the cancellation of major infrastructural projects, such as the new Willemsbrug (1981), which connects the right bank of the Nieuwe Maas to the Noordereiland, or the construction of the Willemsspoortunnel (railway tunnel, in 1993), a two-and-a-half-kilometer long, four-track tunnel under the Nieuwe Maas. The tunnel is part of the railway connection Breda-Rotterdam and replaces the elevated railway that was opened in 1877. Meanwhile, building took place with an eye for quality and with a stricter policy and vision; Rotterdam presented itself as a city of architecture. One of the most striking examples of this development are the 38 cube houses (1984) by architect Piet Blom, arranged as a roof above the busy Blaak. The municipal library was also built along the Blaak, as early as 1983, designed by Jaap Bakema and Hans Boot. With its steel, brightly colored tubes that run down from the roof, the architecture is reminiscent of the Centre Pompidou in Paris.

## Kop van Zuid

In the early nineties, Riek Bakker, then director of Urban Development, created a master plan for the development and infrastructural access of the so-called Kop van Zuid (literally translated: the Head of South). Important elements of this plan are the connections to the center of Rotterdam via the famous Erasmus Bridge and the subway station Wilhelminaplein, thus creating an urban area with many amenities along the river and residential areas along the inner harbors. Several historic buildings, such as Hotel New York, Café Rotterdam and Las Palmas, were maintained and given a new purpose. Many skyscrapers were built, such as the Maas Tower, the World Port Center, Montevideo and finally the building simply called De Rotterdam (2013) by architect Rem Koolhaas.

QUOTE

**Jules Deelder:**

'In Rotterdam they earn it,
in The Hague they distribute it
and in Amsterdam they squander it.'

## From Gutter to Arch

Where shopping was concerned, the center of Rotterdam was given the so-called Beurstraverse (passage), soon known as the Koopgoot, which actually means 'buying-gutter'. The first pole was driven into the ground in 1994 by Jules Deelder, assisted by Herman Brood and Mayor Bram Peper. The shopping center was designed by Pi de Bruijn and the actual passage was constructed below the street level of the Coolsingel, originally as part of the Beurs subway station. Most shops are located on this lower level, but also some of the stores situated at a higher elevation – such as the department stores De Bijenkorf and C & A – have an entrance here. Opposite the library, the Market Hall was built in 2014, an indoor residential and commercial building, located between the streets Binnenrotte, Hoogstraat and Blaak. It was designed by the architectural firm MVRDV. Because of its shape the building was soon named Koopboog, which translates as Buying-Arch.

DID YOU KNOW?

### Rotterdam city of architecture

Many well-known architectural firms such as Van den Broek & Bakema, Maaskant, Quist, Weeber, OMA (Rem Koolhaas), MVRDV (the first letters of the surnames of the three architects Maas, Van Rijs and De Vries) and Neutelings Riedijk have 'grown up' in Rotterdam. With the Nieuwe Instituut (New Institute), the former Dutch Architecture Institute (NAI), and educational institutions such as the Rotterdam Academy of Architecture, the city occupies a leading position in (inter) national architecture.

## Big, Bigger, Biggest

Rotterdam, if you would include the port activities, is so much bigger than the actual municipality boundaries would suggest. The Nieuwe Waterweg (1872) is a lifeline which must be safe and deep enough for the huge flow of shipping traffic. In 1997, the Maeslantkering (the verb 'keren' means to reverse) was put into operation; a barrier on the border of Het Scheur and the New Waterway near Hoek van Holland. It is part of the Europoort-barrier, the final part of the Delta Works. To have some degree of influence on the surrounding areas, Rotterdam has experimented with the Openbaar Lichaam (public body/organization) Rijnmond, a governing body elected directly by the people, acting between the municipality and the province, and intended to coordinate specific problems at a regional level in the Rijnmond area.

The Openbaar Lichaam Rijnmond started in 1964 as an administrative experiment and existed until 1986. Mayor Wim Thomassen saw Rijnmond as an intermediary to achieve a Greater Rotterdam, referring to the London model. The neighboring municipalities did not trust Rotterdam and therefore also not the concept of Rijnmond. They saw the plans of Rotterdam for its port as a threat to the environment in their communities. Mayor Bram Peper tried again later with the formation of a city-province Rijnmond. A city-province would be better equipped to serve the economic interests of the region – including the world's largest port – across the municipal borders. That would also mean the end of Rotterdam as a city. The mayor thus mobilized the majority of town when – in 1995 – he proposed his ideas to the citizens in a referendum. Almost 90 percent of voters rejected the plan, and the bill was quietly withdrawn. The 'Rotterdam-feeling' proved an insurmountable obstacle. Giving up their city? Never!

Was the fear of the neighboring municipalities justified? Annexations of neighboring municipalities or voluntary affiliation often happened in the history of Rotterdam. The most recent one was in 2008. With a narrow majority of the town council of Rozenburg it was decided on July 10, 2008, to dissolve the municipality because of insufficient administrative and political capacity and merge with Rotterdam as a newly formed district. Rozenburg, the smallest municipality in the Netherlands when judged by its surface, is the only place on the island Rozenburg. The village is enclosed by the industry of the Botlek area and Europoort, which covers the entire island. On March 19, 2014, the dissolution of the sub-municipalities was confirmed. They were replaced by fourteen area committees.

DID YOU KNOW?

## Rotterdam in music

Songs about the history of Rotterdam with images from the Municipal Archives: they've been put on DVD by the band The Amazing Stroopwafels – formed in 1979 – and their singer Wim Kerkhof. It doesn't get more authentic than that! Although ... 'Rotterdam' by Frédérique Spigt is obviously a true classic. And if you think about it, there's actually an amazing number of artists originating from Rotterdam: Ntjam Rosie, Sabrina Starke, Dave von Raven from The Kik, Lee Towers, Gerard Cox, Joke Bruijs, Shirma Rouse ... just too many to mention.

## Jules Deelder: Rotown Magic

Rotterdam cannot be captured,

Too soon the images are gone,

Rotterdam just has no past,

And stepped gables there are none.

(...)

It isn't sensitive to the camera,

It doesn't seem more than it is,

It lies square and high and jagged,

Tilted against the glaring light.

(...)

# Experiments

Despite economic setbacks the city still prospers in the period 1970-2015. Yet, during the seventies, the political and social discontent increases. Labour-mayor Thomassen was still around to witness the change. Residents protested vehemently against the demolition of old neighborhoods. Wim Thomassen was succeeded by Labour-politicians André van der Louw (1974-1981) and Bram Peper (1982-1999), the liberal Ivo Opstelten (1999-2008) and Ahmed Aboutaleb (2009-present), again of the Labour Party. The Labour Party (PvdA) prevailed in Rotterdam, but became somewhat estranged from her own supporters. Most people had their daily meals and a regular pint and no longer cared much for major social issues, although the dockworkers still spoke up quite frequently. However, the problem of prostitution in Katendrecht was rather exciting. Around 1970, sex cinemas, theaters and shops came to Katendrecht and ultimately also prostitutes. All this caused much inconvenience to the residents. In April 1971, the Katendrecht neighborhood committee complained in an open letter to the town council. In May and November of 1971, the local government promised that the police would intensify supervision of the area and a ban was issued for soliciting by daylight. In the summer of 1973, the continuous tensions led to a major clash between residents and the local sex industry, resulting in beatings, arson, threats and shots being fired. In February 1975, the mayor and members of the council decided to curb the prostitution in Katendrecht and move the sex business to other sites in Rotterdam. After years of quarreling, the last sex places in Katendrecht were closed in 1981. If the city still wanted to tolerate prostitution, the most important question would be: where? The plans for an 'Eros-center' in the Poortgebouw (Gatehouse) at the Stieltjesstraat met with fierce resistance. These plans were the responsibility of Mayor Van der Louw, whose image eventually appeared on a protest poster in 1979, with a knot tied in his rather large 'Euromast'.

### Tweede Maasvlakte

The Tweede Maasvlakte (literally translated: the Second Maas Plain) is located west of the first Maasvlakte and it is a 2000-hectare expansion project to be realized in the North Sea. On September 1, 2008, the project was launched after years of planning, discussions and protests (mainly environmental). On May 22, 2013, the Tweede Maasvlakte was officially inaugurated.

## Urban Initiatives

The citizens of Rotterdam are not always 'against everything'. In 1989, the residents of the W.C. Opzoomerstraat in the sub-municipality of Delfshaven initiated a make-over of their neighborhood. They paid particular attention to safety, friendly-looking surroundings and clean streets. The project received a lot of media attention and was subsequently supported by the municipality of Rotterdam. 'Opzoomeren' (named after the street) thus grew into a wide-spread project for the whole of Rotterdam. Bram Peper was the mayor who had this project thrown on his doorstep. At the time it actually fitted well within the political aim of striving towards a smaller government with space for citizen-participation and citizens' initiatives.

In recent years the local government has also encouraged people to submit their initiatives, plans for improving and beautifying the city. Thus the Luchtsingel (a raised walkway) came into being, connecting the north of Rotterdam to the city center from the Schiekade. This project brings new life to a forgotten area by means of a bridge, a large roof garden, an entertainment venue at the Hofbogen and a park. The Luchtsingel will actually lead you to the front door of the City Archives of Rotterdam at the Hofdijk, where you can dive into the history of the city (or you can check: www. stadsarchief.rotterdam.nl).

### Festival City

Rotterdam has built up quite a reputation as a festival city. Since the beginning of the seventies, Poetry International/ Dunya and the International Film Festival have been annual events. The Summer Carnival has existed since 1984 and the Gergiev Festival since 1996. Monaco on the Maas has been around since 2005 and the North Sea Jazz Festival since 2006. In 2001, Rotterdam was the Cultural Capital of Europe.

### The North Sea Jazz Festival

In 2006, the North Sea Jazz Festival – organized by impresario Paul Acket – moved from The Hague to Rotterdam, back to its place of origin. Already in 1966, Acket started the three-day jazz festival Newport in Rotterdam, in collaboration with De Doelen. In 1976, Acket moved the event to The Hague because the entertainment tax had just been abolished there.

## Politician Pim Fortuyn

Pim Fortuyn (1948-2002) was an openly gay politician and leader of a movement who opposed the old established politics with the slogan 'that he says what he thinks and does what he promises'. Fortuyn was an Extraordinary Professor (in the field of employment conditions in the civil service) from 1990 to 1995 at the Erasmus University. From 1998 onwards, he lived at the G.W. Burgerplein 11 and he called his house the 'Palazzo di Pietro'. As a publicist and columnist, he powerfully presented himself in the media. He became a celebrity whose beliefs found favor with a wide audience. Fortuyn pointed out the weaknesses of the Dutch system, in which he saw especially the bureaucracy, education, multiculturalism, Islam and the deterioration of neighborhoods in big cities as weak spots. He called for the return of values. With his often provocative stands on these subjects he aroused indignation but also inspired discussions. In 2001, Fortuyn astonished everyone when – on national television – he announced his ambition to become prime minister of the Netherlands. For tactical reasons he also joined the party Leefbaar (livable) Rotterdam. With this party, he achieved a tremendous victory in the municipal elections of March 6, 2002, winning 17 seats. With his List Pim Fortuyn he was preparing for the parliamentary elections of May 15, 2002. In the heat of the national political campaign he was killed on May 6, 2002, at the Media Park in Hilversum. Even without their deceased party leader, the List Pim Fortuyn won 26 seats during the elections! Mayor Ivo Opstelten showed himself a true mayor and father of his citizens when he calmed down the city of Rotterdam in these turbulent days.

DID YOU KNOW?

## Statue of Fortuyn

A statue in memory of Pim Fortuyn was unveiled in front of the Schielandshuis on May 6, 2003. The 4.5-meter high statue, made by the artist Corry Ammerlaan, also from Rotterdam, was donated to the municipality by the foundation 'Statue of Pim'. On the pedestal is the saying 'Loquendi Libertatem Custodiamus' (Latin for 'Let us guard the freedom of speech').

## Remembering

The bombing was never far away in the memory of the citizens of Rotterdam, if only because of the many empty spaces in the city. The port had been repaired, the city rebuilt and economic relations restored. Gradually, more attention was paid to the victims of the war, who saw their despair represented in the famous statue by Zadkine called De Verwoeste Stad (The Destroyed City) – also known as 'City without a heart' or 'Jan Gat' (John Hole). In the city itself the commemoration of the war took more shape in 2006 when 'Initiative May 14' was founded, with the goal of giving more content and meaning to the commemoration of May 14, 1940. There has been no long remembrance tradition to speak of.

## Fire boundary

The area of Rotterdam that was devastated by the German bombardment of May 14, 1940, and the subsequent fires is known as the Brandgrens (Fire Boundary). The old center has disappeared and unlike in most other Dutch cities the link with the past is barely visible. Since 2010, the 12-km long fire boundary is permanently marked using beautifully designed lights in the pavement. The fire boundary has thus become a lasting memory, but also a means to understand the city better. Rotterdam is an old city with a young heart. The physical marking of the fire boundary has a virtual counterpart: www.brandgrens.nl. On this website you can find everything about Rotterdam during the Second World War, including interviews with witnesses. The site also offers the possibility of downloading city walks along the fire boundary. During these walks you can witness the connection between old and new, the line between preserved and devastated areas.

The marking of the fire boundary consists of 400 lights in the pavement. Together they form a line of light indicating until where the flames reached after the bombing. Each light contains an image with the silhouette of a Heinkel bomber, burning houses and the statue 'Destroyed City' by Zadkine. The design was realized by the agency West 8 in collaboration with Opera Graphic Design.

# Chapter 10

# Ten unforgettable buildings

***In This Chapter:***

- The White House
- Van Nelle Factory
- Feyenoord Stadium
- Groothandelsgebouw
- Euromast
- Blaakse Bos
- Hotel New York
- Erasmus Bridge
- Rotterdam Central Station
- Markthal

## *1898: National Heritage Site The White House*

At one time, Het Witte Huis (The White House) at the Geldersekade, with its ten floors, was the first skyscraper in Europe, which it remained for decades. The White House was designed by the brothers Herman and Gerrit van der Schuijt. During his trip to New York, Gerrit was struck by the impressive skyscrapers. Back in Rotterdam, he realized his building-ideas together with architect Willem Molenbroek. Construction on the White House was started in 1897. Because an adjacent building collapsed during the process of driving the piles into the ground, the floor size was eventually reduced from 20 by 20 meters to 20 by 15 meters. Hundred piles were used for the foundation. The 45-meter high building has no steel structure, as used in American skyscrapers, but is actually a brick tower. The viewing platform and the floors, three of which are located under the sloping roof, can be accessed via electric cage elevators, a novelty at the time. Nowadays, the viewing platform is open only during events.

**Figure 10.1:** The Wijnhaven (Wine Harbor) with the White House; postcard from 1898

The White House, which survived the bombing, was built in the Art Nouveau style, which is particularly visible in the white glazed tile panels covering the building on the outside above the windows. The tiles display elegantly shaped plant and floral motifs. They were manufactured by the Faience- en Tegelfabriek Holland in Utrecht. On the east side of the Geldersekade, a large tile panel carries the name of the building. The niches contain sculptures made in 1898 by the Rotterdam sculptor Simon Miedema. They represent the personifications of Agriculture and Industry, Labor and Progress and Commerce and Navigation. During the battle for the

Willemsbrug in May 1940, shrapnel destroyed the statue of Labor. Navigation was later put in its place, leaving the north side with an empty niche.

## 1924-1931: World Heritage Site Van Nelle Factory

The Van Nelle Factory is one of the icons of the architectural movement Nieuwe Bouwen (New Building) in the Netherlands. The company, in full called De weduwe (widow) J. van Nelle, bought some land along the Delfhavense Schie in 1916, located in the municipality then called Overschie, now the Spaanse Polder. They wanted to build a new factory for coffee, tea and tobacco, but only after the site had grown to measure some 90,000 square meters, suitable for a new factory, work began on the reclamation of the polder, in 1924. This was done with silt from the newly dug Merwehaven. Already in 1917, Kees van der Leeuw was appointed co-partner of Van Nelle, with the special task of developing a new factory complex. The architect Michiel Brinkman was commissioned to design the new building, but due to his untimely death in 1925, his son Jan Brinkman took over the assignment. Jan Brinkman then started working with architect Leendert van der Vlugt. Both were supporters of the Nieuwe Bouwen. According to the principles of this architectural movement light, air and space played an important role. These elements were realized using modern materials and construction methods. Much attention was also paid to the labor circumstances. The driving of reinforced concrete piles was an unknown practice in the Netherlands, which meant that a lot of pioneering work needed to be done. In 1928, the tobacco factory was finished, but other parts, such as the boiler room and the office building, still had to be built. However, the plans had to be adjusted because of the stock market crash in New York in 1929. Eventually, the entire plant was completed in 1931.

The building has a concrete structure with mushroom-shaped columns, which meant that the non-load-bearing walls could be made almost entirely of glass. The façades let in a huge amount of light. By means of high-level bridges with conveyor belts, the factory was connected with the shipping and storage spaces along the water. The tobacco factory is centrally located and with its height of eight floors and a length of 220 meters it is the highest building of the complex. It was Van der Vlugt who came up with the idea to provide the tobacco factory with a view/tearoom in the form of a chocolate box.

Wessel de Jonge Architects transformed the Van Nelle Factory (in 1998) into a 'Design Factory'. It now accommodates creative companies and offers space for congresses and meetings. In June, 2014, the Van Nelle Factory was added to the list of UNESCO World Heritage Sites.

## 1937: Feyenoord Stadium

The Feyenoord Stadium actually has the same architects as the Van Nelle Factory: Brinkman and Van der Vlugt. In the midst of the crisis, on September 16, 1935, the first pile was driven into the ground by the football player Puck van Heel. The stadium came into being largely due to the financial support of a number of Rotterdam residents, such as the industrial magnate D.G. van Beuningen and banker K.P. van der Mandele. It was built in the part of town called Zuid (South), on an undeveloped plot of land along the Maas. The stadium could accommodate 61,500 people at the time. Like the Van Nelle factory, this stadium was also built according to the principles of the Nieuwe Bouwen movement. The open exterior exhibits a self-supporting steel structure with stands, landings, and a roof in which the crossbeams (or rafters) are connected to each other by means of iron purlins. Characteristic is the oval arena, in which the seats are divided in an upper and lower stand, instead of the usual stands that slope upward in a straight line. It creates an unobstructed view for all spectators. Because of its shape, very soon the stadium became known as 'De Kuip' (the Tub).

## 1953: National Heritage Site Groothandelsgebouw

In 1953, the 35-meter high and 220-meter long Groothandelsgebouw (Trade Building) was completed. Designed by the architects H.A. Maaskant and W. van Tijen it was the tallest building in Western Europe. It was built on the former location of the Zoo, which had already been moved to Blijdorp before the war. After an idea of wholesaler Frits Pot, the choice was made for one large business complex instead of dozens of small premises. Pot realized that it would be easier to get a license for one large building than for dozens of buildings of individual wholesalers. The Groothandelsgebouw would accommodate some hundred companies. For the most efficient transport of products the building possessed an interior street for trucks. Atop the building stood in big letters the word 'Groothandelsgebouw', indicating that it was a building for wholesale (groothandel in Dutch, gebouw means building). Several years ago the name was changed to 'Groot Handelsgebouw' which is actually a misnomer (as that would mean Large Trade Building). Typical of the building is the grid structure of concrete columns on which the building rests, which produced many effective square meters.

Already during the process of construction several companies settled in the building, such as grand café and conference center Engels. In 1961, the roof was also put into use with the establishment of movie theater Kriterion. Before the start of the movie and during breaks, the screen was pulled up to give the audience – by means of a glass wall – a view of the city under construction.

# 1960: Euromast

In 1955, the idea was introduced to build a high tower at the Parkhaven. Since the municipality of Rotterdam would not contribute financially, the committee 'Rotterdamse Uitkijktoren in oprichting' (roughly translated Rotterdam Watchtower development) declared that even without the aid of municipal finances it would still build the tower. The municipality did, however, make the necessary building site available. In 1958, the committee announced that the tower would be finished at the opening of the International Horticultural Exhibition Floriade in 1960. The contract was awarded to architect H.A. Maaskant. He designed a tower with only a single vantage point, the Crow's Nest, at 100 meters altitude. According to Maaskant this was the ideal height so that visitors could still distinguish traffic and people from a distance. Moreover, in case of bad weather the tower still had to be an attractive goal for visitors. The concrete shaft was constructed on the spot sitting atop a foundation slab with a capacity of 3.8 million kilograms. The steel 'bridge' and the Kraaiennest (Crow's Nest) were manufactured elsewhere. The Kraaiennest was mounted at the base of the mast, and then hoisted up along the shaft in five days. After that the 'bridge' was attached to the shaft. The entrance was the last part of the tower to be finished. The construction took a period of fourteen months. On March 25, 1960, when the Floriade was opened by Princess Beatrix, the Euromast was also opened to the public.

Two elevators in the shaft brought the visitors to the Crow's Nest. The visual dynamics of the tower are created by the asymmetry of the Crow's Nest, which has a maximum diameter of 29 meters. Located along the Parkhaven, the Euromast was an important landmark at the time, both from the water and in the city. With its 101 meters, the Euromast used to be the tallest building in the Netherlands until the Medical Faculty was built, standing 14 meters taller. But the Euromast regained the top position when the 84-meter high Space Tower was added to it. The Space Tower is a steel cylinder with a diameter of 2.5 meters, around which a revolving elevator was constructed. From the Crow's Nest a hydraulic elevator brings the visitor to the elevator cabin of the Space Tower which is located 8 meters higher. With its now 185 meters the Euromast was again the highest construction in the Netherlands. Since 2005 it is legally allowed to use the tower for rappelling (abseiling), skydiving and base jumping.

## 1984: Blaakse Bos

The bombed area Oudehaven/Groenendaal had been an empty and desolate part of town for years, which was a thorn in the side of many locals. In 1974 the decision was taken to build homes that would attract more affluent citizens, instead of opting for more offices, retail buildings and social housing. However, the problem was that – towards the city center – the area was bisected by the Blaak, one of Rotterdam's busiest traffic roads. Nevertheless, the Spaansekade and the Markt would have to be connected, as had been the case in history. The municipality of Rotterdam wanted to create something special for this extraordinary place – the oldest part of the city, where the original town of Rotterdam had emerged at the confluence of the Rotte and the river Maas. The architect chosen for the job was Piet Blom – from Amsterdam – who was elected based on his stilt houses (or tree houses) in Helmond.

The project had a turbulent building history, in which one after the other developer pulled out. The project was finally realized in 1984. A total of 38 cube houses were built on the Blaak – which had a height difference of about 6 meters with the surrounding area. The interlocking cubes each rest on concrete trunks, thus looking like a stylized forest and hence the name Blaakse Bos (bos means forest). From the beginning it was clear that the Blaakse Bos would not be positively received by everyone. The sloping walls of the cube houses make sure that almost nothing from an ordinary house fits in. The houses demand a lot from the inhabitants' creativity, but on the other hand they are in the heart of Rotterdam. The project also included the Blaaktoren, a striking residential tower at the Binnenrotte, nicknamed Het Potlood (the Pencil) and also designed by Piet Blom.

## (1917) 1993: Hotel New York

On May 5, 1993, Council member J.M. Linthorst officially opened the Hotel New York, situated in the former office of the Holland America Line (HAL) at the Wilhelminakade. The headquarters had fallen into disuse after the HAL – in 1989 – had become part of the US company Carnival Corporation & plc in Seattle. The executive office, which was opened in 1917, was designed by the architects Muller, Droogleever Fortuyn and Van der Tak. The solid block was adorned with Art Nouveau ornaments and two characteristic turrets, which were added a bit later. During the bombing of May 14, 1940, most of the buildings on the pier were destroyed. A single warehouse and the main office were spared. The architects Van den Broek and Bakema designed one large departure hall for the area, the current Cruise Terminal – and a workshop for the HAL – currently Las Palmas. Yet it became increasingly quiet along the Wilhelminakade, especially after the HAL had stopped its regular service to New York in 1971. HAL remained in business until 1978, but finally closed her office in 1984. The area was facing a bleak future until the municipality commissioned the development of urban plans for the Kop van Zuid, as the area was called. Along the Wilhelminakade many high-rise buildings were planned, which gave the press a reason to speak of 'Manhattan on the Maas'. Hotel New York – opened in 1993 – became a major attraction. By now the Hotel is surrounded by high-rise buildings, such as the 124-meter tall World Port Center, the first tower building of the area, and the residential towers Montevideo, Maastoren, New Orleans and – most recently – the municipal office De Rotterdam, opened in 2013.

# 1996: Erasmus Bridge

The Erasmus Bridge, designed by Ben van Berkel, is the second bridge across the Nieuwe Maas besides the Willemsbrug. It was officially opened on September 4, 1996, by Queen Beatrix and immediately became a landmark in the city. The imposing bridge connects the Kop van Zuid to the city center on the other side of the river. The 802-meter long cable-stayed bridge has a 139-meter asymmetric steel pylon, from which the bridge earned its nickname The Swan. From its peak, heavy cables descend to the deck of the bridge. While the Erasmus Bridge was being constructed, the spaces next to it – on the quay – were filled in as well. The office of Spido Rondvaarten (city cruise boats) was established at this location, and so were a restaurant and a parking garage. Shortly after the opening there was a moment of panic when – while a wind of Beaufort force 6 was blowing – the bridge unexpectedly began to sway and the cables started to tremble. The problems were solved by installing new shock absorbers. On January 26, 2010, the bridge was back in the news. It had to be closed as a large lump of ice situated at the top of the bridge threatened to fall down. The block of ice was thawed by two heating elements that had been installed at the top of the bridge, allowing it to be opened again the next day. All kinds of events take place around the bridge, such as the Red Bull Air Race Rotterdam and the World Port Days. The route of the Marathon Rotterdam crosses the bridge and so did the Tour de France on July 3, 2010.

# 2014: Rotterdam Central Station

The Central Station was officially opened by King Willem-Alexander on May 13, 2014. Before the Second World War, Rotterdam used to have no less than four stations in and around the center, each with different destinations. That problem was solved by building a central station, designed by the architect Sybold van Ravesteyn, which was officially opened on May 21, 1957. It actually replaced the Delftse

Poort Station, which had been badly damaged during the bombing of Rotterdam. But after fifty years this particular station by Van Ravesteyn had become too small. It was closed in 2007 and demolition works began in 2008. From the old and distinctive letters 'Central Station' the design studio Bureau Lakenvelder put together the words 'Traan Laten' (crying) which prominently adorned the building to be demolished. This was a way of indicating that the citizens of Rotterdam parted with the reconstruction monument somewhat against their will.

ProRail and the Municipality of Rotterdam gave the assignment for the design of the new station to Team CS, a cooperation between Benthem Crouwel Architects, MVSA Meyer & Van Schooten Architects, and West 8. Years of hassle and annoyances made the citizens of Rotterdam critical towards the project. Their uneasy attitude had been unnecessary. Upon completion, the new building was quickly embraced and almost everyone loved it. The so-called 'speculaasjes' (a Dutch kind of cookie), artworks that had adorned the wings of the old railway station, now stand above the end of the bicycle tunnel. At the special request of the residents of Rotterdam the old clock and the words 'Central Station' by Van Ravesteyn returned to the rear side of the station.

## 2014: Markthal

The Market Hall, an indoor residential and shopping building, is located between the Binnenrotte, Hoogstraat and Blaak. The complex was officially opened by Queen Máxima on October 1, 2014. In addition to an indoor market, the building consists of 228 apartments, 4600 square meters of retail space, 1600 square meters of restaurants and other food and drink locations and a car park for more than a thousand cars. The Market Hall was designed by MVRDV Architects. The gray stone building has the shape of a horseshoe. On both ends the Market Hall has glass façades. The inner wall is covered with an 11,000 square meter large artwork by Arno

Coenen, titled 'Horn of Plenty', referring to the Cornucopia, the horn of Greek mythology symbolizing abundance and saturation. The artwork shows greatly enlarged pieces of fruit, vegetables, ears of wheat, flowers, fish and insects. People already call it 'the Sistine Chapel of Rotterdam'. Other names for the building itself are 'Buying-Arch' or 'Pencil Sharpener'. During construction works, a tenth-century farm was excavated at seven meters below street level, belonging to the original settlement of Rotta. The excavated objects are now visible in the so-called Tijdtrap (Time Staircase) in the stairwell of the parking garage. The Market Hall has become a huge tourist attraction for visitors from both home and abroad.

# Index